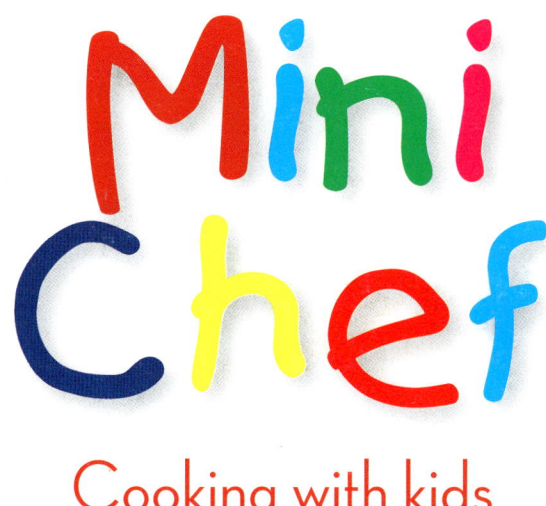

Mini Chef

Cooking with kids

Sheridan Rogers

NEW HOLLAND

To my children, Natali and Linden, and
to all the children who attend my kids cooking
classes and bring me joy.

acknowledgements

I'd like to extend my thanks to the following people: Kim Anderson for her encouragement and support, stylist Mandy Biffin for her flair and attention to detail, photographer Graeme Gillies, project editor Rochelle Fernandez for her patience and designer Emma Gough.

Thanks to Paula Weekes and Wendy Thomson for their support and assistance and to all the beautiful enthusiastic children (and their parents) who appear in the book: Jamie and Jade Everett, Claudia Spirou, Joss and Louis Merrill.

A big thank you to Andy Allegaert, My Little Cupcake, 62 Ben Boyd Road, Neutral Bay, NSW. www.mylittlecupcake.com.au

The cupcakes and props on pages 42, mixmaster on pages 70, 134, 128, 143, 152, 158 are from: My Little Cupcake, Sarah Gardener, Burnt Orange, 1108/1109 Middle Head Road, Mosman, NSW. www.burntorange.com.au, Justine Joffe, Retrospections, 498a Miller St, Cammeray, NSW. justine@retrospections.com.au

Thank you to Janice Baker and Jerry Rogers for lending so many of their lovely cloths and dishes.

Thanks to to June Factor for quotes from the following books:

Far Out, Brussel Sprout! Children's chants and rhymes (Melbourne University Press 1983)

Unreal, Banana Peel! A third collection of Australian children's chants and rhymes. (Melbourne University Press 1986)

Roll Over, Pavlova! A fifth collection of Australian children's chants and rhymes. (Hodder & Stoughton 1992)

All Right, Vegemite! A new collection of children's chants and rhymes. (Melbourne University Press 1985)

introduction

My son was about seven when he took to messing around in the kitchen, usually on a Sunday morning. I remember some nice surprises—milky cups of tea, burnt pieces of toast, bowls of cereal weighed down by mountains of banana: all offerings of love.

One Sunday, though, he really went to town. At school he'd been reading *George's Marvellous Medicine*, an amusing tale by Roald Dahl, and had decided to concoct a potent brew similar to George's.

I recall my nine-year-old daughter, Natali, shrieking, 'Linden, come and turn it off. It's burning!'. I was instantly awake, leapt out of bed and ran down the hall, becoming aware of a ghastly smell, up my nose, in my eyes. I couldn't escape it.

Meanwhile, the culprit was on my bed looking abashed. He'd crept in for an early-morning cuddle ten minutes earlier and had forgotten to turn off a pot on the stove.

Like eight-year-old George in the book, he'd cooked up his own brew. In went a cake of soap, the chilli sauce, the peanut butter, the jar of pesto, a dash of perfume and his Dad's aftershave lotion. Like George, he found a long wooden spoon and began stirring hard. The stuff in the pot got hotter and hotter. But then, unlike George, he left the pot boiling away on the stove and came in for a cuddle.

Well, the fearsome smell certainly got me out of bed (probably his intention all along). But it also made me realise how potentially dangerous it is to let a child muck about in the kitchen with no supervision.

In the cooking classes I run at my home, we have plenty of fun kneading pizza or bread dough, peeling and cutting fruit and vegetables, checking out the vegies and herbs in my garden, and cooking and baking—but there's always an adult present.

When I was a child, my Sundays were often spent cooking with my mother or one of my aunts. My parents entertained a lot and there were always plenty of people around who were keen to try our latest creations. My mother was an adventurous cook and appreciated having a 'little helper' by her side.

I didn't need much encouragement because the enticing smells and warmth emanating from the kitchen were like a magnet to me. I especially loved baking and would always volunteer to help with making cakes: creaming the butter and sugar, breaking the eggs, sifting the flour, grating an orange and squeezing its juice to make an orange cake; or rubbing together the butter and flour to make pastry for an apple or date pie. I loved the sensuality of it, the touching, tasting, smelling, pounding, pouring and shaping which resulted in something delicious to eat.

My mother would also involve me in the shopping, taking my sister and me with her to the central markets on Saturday mornings to purchase the weekly fruit, vegetables, meat and fish. I loved these excursions because the market was a very lively place and introduced me to a completely different world, one in which Chinese market gardeners, Italian grocers and Greek fishermen competed for our attention.

We rarely needed to buy fresh herbs or leafy greens such as parsley, lettuce or silverbeet because my father grew these in his vegetable patch at home.

The ability to cook, and to grow our own herbs and leafy greens are important life skills and one of the most important things we can pass on to children. Knowing how to cook a nutritious meal is not just important for keeping body and soul together, it's also a valuable social asset because it encourages self-confidence and independence—and friends and family will always appreciate a home-cooked meal, especially one made with confidence and love.

contents

ready, set, GO!

READY...

1. Do you have all the ingredients?
2. Wash your hands—no one likes dirty hands when cooking.
3. Put on a t-shirt and apron so you don't mess up your clothes. And don't forget your shoes (such as runners) in case something falls on your toes.
4. If you have long hair, tie it up. You'll look good, there won't be any hair in your food and no chance of it catching fire.
5. Check the bench-top is clear before you start, and wipe down surfaces, clearing up as you go along. Boring but you'll never be a pro otherwise.
6. Wash and dry all fruits and vegetables before you use them. Even the freshest fruit and veg need a quick rinse.
7. Defrost meat, poultry or seafood in the refrigerator, on a plate lined with paper towels. A MUST! Have you ever had food poisoning?
8. If you're in a hurry, you can also use the microwave. But remember, no aluminium foil and be careful that it's not in there too long to actually cook the meat! A slow defrost is all you need.
9. Clean up as you go. Cleaning up isn't so bad when you do it as you go.

SET...

10. Before you start cooking, read the recipe carefully. Does it make sense?

11. And do you have enough time?

12. Check that you have all the necessary ingredients. Place the ingredients that you need on the bench-top—this is especially important when stir-frying as all the food needs to be cooked quickly. The French call this *mise en place* (pronounced 'meez on plahs') which means measuring and chopping the ingredients listed in the recipe before you start cooking.

13. Use the timer on your oven—it's the one piece of equipment all mini chefs can't do without it. Otherwise a kitchen timer is very handy and will help to remind you when things are ready.

GO !

measuring

Try not to lose count (as Alice did in Through the Looking Glass!*)
when you are measuring ingredients.*

Wet ingredients
Butter:
1. A block of butter weighs 250g (8oz). Most wrappers are marked with measuring lines—use a sharp knife to cut off the correct amount.
2. Or, weigh the butter on digital scales—place it in a plastic container or tray which has been placed on the scales and set on zero.

Liquids
1. Use measuring cups to measure liquid ingredients. Pour in the liquid until it comes to the top.
2. Or, you can use a glass or plastic measuring jug. Pour in the liquid while bending down so that measuring lines are at eye level and you can see that the liquid reaches the line.

Dry ingredients

1. Spoon dry ingredients such as flour and sugar into dry measuring cups or spoons.
2. Level off with the back of a knife. Do not pack down unless you are measuring brown sugar which is always firmly packed.
3. Or you can measure dry ingredients on digital scales. Spoon ingredients into a plastic container which has been placed on the scales and set on zero.

baking

1. Place mixing bowl on a damp cloth—this will prevent it from moving around on the benchtop.
2. When mixing, use a spatula to scrape down sides of bowl. Beat again to combine mixture.
3. When whisking egg whites, the bowl must be clean and dry, otherwise the whites won't form peaks.
4. Make sure you use the right tin as specified in the recipe. Line base and sides of tins with baking paper—a little softened butter rubbed onto the tin will help hold it in place.
5. Testing for 'done-ness': insert a skewer into the middle of the cake—if no mixture sticks to it, the cake is ready. If there is still some mixture on the skewer, it needs a little longer in the oven.
6. Use oven mitts to lift cake from oven. Leave in tin for 5–10 minutes or as specified then turn out onto a cake rack.

"We're going to make a cake,
we're going to make a cake;
We're going to make it really big,
because we all like cake.

Flour in the bowl, flour in the bowl;
Stir it with a great big spoon,
Flour in the bowl."

~ Children's chant

how to...

Separate eggs

1. Always break eggs into a cup first. If one is bad, you can throw it out without ruining the mixture. If there's any shell in the egg, the easiest way to remove it is to scoop it out with a larger piece of shell.

2. Crack egg on side of a small bowl, aiming to hit the bowl with the middle of the egg or use the back of a kitchen knife to gently tap the shell.

3. Using the two halves of the shell, transfer the yolk from one half to another, letting the white drop into the bowl. Place yolk in a small cup.

4. You can also use your hands, but make sure they are clean first! Crack the egg on the side of a small bowl, and, holding your hand over the bowl, allow the white to slip through your fingers into the bowl. Place yolk in a small cup.

Melt chocolate

1. Roughly chop or break chocolate into squares and place in a heatproof bowl.

2. Place bowl over a saucepan of simmering water—check that the bottom is not touching the water.

3. Stir occasionally until melted and glossy. Remove bowl immediately from heat.

Toast nuts

Toasted nuts add flavour and crunch to all your dishes.

1. Spread the quantity you require on a baking tray and roast in a preheated moderate oven for about 10 minutes. Watch carefully to ensure they don't burn.

2. If using hazelnuts, rub their skins off in a tea towel using the palms of your hands.

Roast capsicum

1. Cut capsicums in half then into quarters. Cut out the white membranes and discard the seeds.
2. Place capsicum quarters skin-side-up on an oven tray lined with baking paper.
3. Heat oven or grill to moderate and cook prepared capsicums until skin begins to blister and burn. Remove tray. Use tongs to put capsicum pieces in a plastic bag.
4. Leave 10–15 minutes or until cool, then peel away the skin.

Crush garlic

1. Separate garlic cloves from the head (bulb) of garlic.
2. Place clove of garlic on chopping board. Use the flat side of a heavy knife to press down firmly or smash each clove (this makes it easy to remove the skin).
3. Cut the clove lengthways. If there is a green shoot, discard it because it is bitter.
4. Crush the clove in a garlic press or mortar and pestle with salt, or chop it finely, depending on your recipe.

Peel tomatoes

1. Using a small sharp knife, make a shallow cross in the base of the tomato.
2. Bring a small pan of water to boiling point. Fill a medium bowl with cold water.
3. Place the tomato in the boiling water for one minute. Remove with a slotted spoon and place immediately into the bowl of cold water.
4. Starting from the base, loosen the skin with the knife and peel away.

how to...

vegetables

Onions

Some of the children in my classes tell me they use goggles when chopping onions. Or you could be really cool and wear sunglasses!

1. Place onion on chopping board and cut in half lengthways, cut off the top end, then peel skin off both halves (some onion skins are quite thick, so you might need to remove several layers).
2. Slice each half thinly lengthways without cutting through the root.
3. Now slice through from top to bottom holding slices together at the root end. Watch your fingers!
4. Cut across the slices to make chopped pieces. If not fine enough, chop through some more. Discard the root end.
5. Or—and this is the easy way—cut onion in half, peel and cut into quarters. Chop in the food processor.

Leeks

1. Chop root end and green leaves off leek so that there is just the white part left.
2. Slice the leek and rinse under running water in a strainer before using because leeks can retain soil. Dry on paper towels before proceeding.

Carrots

1. Hold carrot at thick top end and use a vegetable peeler to peel the skin. Push the peeler away from you while you keep turning and peeling. Wash well. Chop off the top and bottom of the carrot and wash it.

- For carrot slices: place carrot on chopping board and cut even slices, starting at thin end and moving your fingers backwards from the knife. Be careful—carrots love to roll around.

- For carrot sticks: use peeled thick top end only. Cut carrot in half lengthways and sit the halves flat on the board. Cut into thin slices, then cut across into matchstick-size pieces (batons). Once you have matchsticks, you can chop neatly into dice-size pieces. Even easier is to let the food processor do the chopping.
- For shredded carrot, use a grater.

Potatoes

Choose potatoes which have no sprouts and are not green.

1. Use a vegetable peeler to peel the skin, pushing the peeler away from you. Wash the potatoes well.

2. Place potato on a chopping board and cut in half lengthways. Cut into quarters and then into eighths.

- For sliced potatoes: cut a thin slice off the potato so it sits firmly on the chopping board. Slice to desired thickness, moving your fingers backwards from the knife.

Garden herbs

Herbs add flavour to your food and help you to rely less on salt for tastiness.

1. Choose the herbs from your garden that you need and pick off the leaves. Wash well and pat dry using a tea towel.
2. Place leaves on a chopping board. Hold the knife with one hand and place the fingers of your other hand on top of the knife.
3. Rock knife back and forth to chop the leaves.

Lettuces/mixed baby green leaves

1. Wash green leaves in a salad spinner: place leaves in basket and cover with water. Leave to stand for a couple of minutes.
2. Drain the basket of water in the sink. Tip out any excess water.
3. Spin the leaves, using cord on salad spinner, until dry.
4. To separate iceberg lettuce leaves: remove dark outer green leaves and remove core of lettuce with a small sharp knife. Gently bang core-end face down on chopping board to loosen leaves, then place under a tap of running cold water to force outer leaves off in one piece.

Corn

1. Peel off the husk and remove all the silky threads—this is easier if you do it under running water.
2. Place flat end of corn on chopping board. Starting at the top, run the knife down the corn so that the kernels fall onto the board.
3. Keep rotating the corn until all the kernels have come off. Repeat with other piece of corn.

Chop, chop, choppity-chop,
Cut off the bottom
And cut off the top;
What there's left we will
Put in the pot;
Chop, chop, choppity-chop.
children guess which vegetables can
be chopped like this: carrots, onions...

– Children's Chant

fruit

Apples and pears

1. Place apple or pear on a chopping board. Use a vegetable peeler to peel away skin from top to bottom, pushing peeler away from you. Keep turning the fruit until all the skin has been taken off.
2. To core apples or pear: cut in half from top to bottom, then cut into quarters. Using a small knife, cut out core from each quarter. Cut into fine slices or dice.
3. If you are not using the fruit immediately, brush it with lemon juice to prevent browning.

Stone fruit (peaches, apricots, plums, nectarines)

1. To peel: Follow instructions for peeling tomatoes (in vegetables).
2. Cut peach or apricot in half along the indentation.
3. Twist the two halves apart gently.
4. Using a teaspoon, lift out the stone

Passionfruit

1. Cut passionfruit in half with a small sharp knife.
2. Scoop out pulp and seeds with a teaspoon. Freeze in ice cube trays when in season so you always have some pulp on hand.

Strawberries

1. Wash strawberries then cut off their hulls (the green at the top) and slice or dice, according to your recipe.
2. If you are making chocolate-dipped strawberries, leave the hull on and don't wash them.

Citrus (oranges, lemons, tangelos, grapefruit, limes)

1. To extract as much juice as possible from citrus fruits, place in a bowl of hot water for a minute, then roll gently backwards and forwards on the bench top.
2. To zest, use a microplane or zester or smallest holes on your grater. Rotate the fruit frequently and don't press too hard as you want rind only, not the white pith. Make sure you zest citrus fruits before you juice them.
3. For strips (or julienne) of citrus: ask an adult to help you peel the rind with a small sharp knife. Cut off any white pith. Cut rind into very fine strips and use to decorate fruit salads and cakes.

Avocado

1. Cut the avocado in half lengthways around the seed then give both halves a firm twist in different directions. Use a dessertspoon to pull out the seed.
2. Place cut halves face down on chopping board and carefully ease away the skin.

breakfast

'Alice laughed: "There's no use trying," she said, "one can't believe impossible things."
"I daresay you haven't had much practice," said the Queen. "When I was younger, I always did it for half an hour a day. Why, sometimes I've believed as many as six impossible things before breakfast."'

- Alice in Wonderland by Lewis Carroll

Good Morning Eggs

Make these for your parents so that they can lie in on Sunday morning—a really good one to make for Dad on Father's Day. Serve it with a couple of pieces of buttered wholemeal toast.

Preparation time: 10 minutes
Cooking time: 12–15 minutes
Serves: 2

equipment

2 x 185ml (6fl oz) ramekins (small round ovenproof dishes; if you don't have a ramekin dish, use a sturdy coffee cup)
Measuring spoons
Small saucepan
Pastry brush
Scissors
1 medium knife
Grater
Aluminium foil
Small baking tray or cake tin
Jug of hot water

ingredients

1 teaspoon melted butter
2 tablespoons diced ham or bacon pieces
1 tablespoon snipped chives (i.e. cut with scissors)
2 free range or organic eggs, at room temperature
2 tablespoons cream (optional)
Freshly ground black pepper
2 tablespoons grated tasty or mozzarella cheese

Tip: You can also add some fresh baby spinach leaves: wash and dry 1/3 cup leaves, tear them into small pieces and add to the bacon at the bottom of the dish.

method

1. Preheat oven to 180°C (160°C fan-forced/350°F/gas mark 4). Brush the ramekins with melted butter.
2. Line the bottom of each ramekin with bacon and chives, then carefully break an egg into each. Top with 1 tablespoon cream (if using), grind over a little pepper then sprinkle with cheese.

*Ask an older sister or brother to help with the next two steps

3. Cover the ramekins with aluminium foil and place in a small baking tray or cake tin. Pour in enough hot water to come ⅓ way up the sides of the ramekins—use a jug to make sure you don't spill any. Place in the oven and bake for 15–20 minutes. Check to see if cooked – the whites should be set and yolk runny. Be careful not to let the eggs become leathery.
4. Serve with hot buttered toast.

Scrambled Eggs on Toast

Scrambled eggs and toast are a good starting point to learn to do two things at the one time. As you'll discover, many more complex dishes mean you have to do two (or three or four) things at once.

Preparation time: 5 minutes
Cooking time: 5 minutes
Per person

equipment

Measuring spoons
Small mixing bowl
Fork or whisk
Small non-stick frying pan
Toaster

ingredients

2 free range or organic eggs
1 tablespoon milk
Salt and freshly ground black
  pepper
2 teaspoons butter
Freshly chopped chives or
  grated cheese (optional)
2 slices toasted bread

method

1. In a medium bowl, whisk together the eggs with the milk, a pinch of salt and some freshly ground black pepper.
2. Melt the butter in a medium non-stick pan, pour in the egg mixture and cook over low heat, stirring until eggs are soft and creamy. Sprinkle with chives or grated cheese, if you like.
3. Serve immediately with pieces of hot buttered toast.

Bircher Muesli

In Roald Dahl's Charlie and the Chocolate Factory*, breakfast cereal was thought to be made from 'curly wooden shavings you find in pencil sharpeners'. Let me assure you this delicious muesli isn't made from wooden shavings. You will need to start making it the night before by soaking the oats in the apple juice. Top it with any fruit you like—sliced peaches, apricots or mangoes in summer; diced pears in autumn or try sliced bananas.*

Preparation time: 10 minutes (plus overnight in refrigerator)
Serves: 2

equipment

Medium small bowl
Measuring cups and spoons
Small knife
Vegetable peeler
Grater

ingredients

1 cup traditional oats or your
   favourite muesli
¾ cup (185ml/6fl oz) apple juice
1 Granny Smith apple, peeled
   and grated
½ cup vanilla or honey yogurt
½ cup mixed berries (diced
   strawberries, blueberries,
   raspberries or 2 tablespoons
   sultanas)
1 tablespoon toasted
   macadamias or almonds,
   roughly chopped

method

1. Place oats or muesli in a medium bowl, pour over the apple juice, cover with plastic wrap and leave in fridge overnight.
2. Just before serving, stir through the grated apple. Top with yoghurt, berries and nuts.

Variations: Use rolled rice for a gluten-free option and soy yogurt or soy milk if you prefer dairy-free.

Flour Power Bread

Making bread is fun, especially if you bake it in flowerpots!

Preparation time: 25 minutes
Rising time: approx. 3 hours
Cooking time: 45 minutes

equipment

Measuring cups and spoons
Wooden spoon
Large mixing bowl
Aluminium foil
Plastic wrap
Tea-towel
Wire rack
4 terracotta flower pots or
  2 loaf tins

Note: Use new terracotta flower pots, about 12cm in height. Soak them in cold water for a few hours then scrub well (don't use detergent!). Dry well then line with baking paper or foil brushed lightly with oil.

ingredients

3½ cups wholemeal flour
3 cups unbleached plain flour
2 teaspoons salt
1 tablespoon raw sugar
1 sachet (2 teaspoons)
  dry yeast
2–3 cups warm water
1 tablespoon olive oil

Tip: Experiment with different shapes and sizes of flower pots.

"This is the way we bake our bread,
We bake our bread, we bake our bread.
This is the way we bake our bread,
So early in the morning."

– Traditional Nursery Rhyme

method

1. Combine the flours, salt and half the sugar in a medium-large bowl. In a small bowl, mix the yeast with ½ cup water and remaining sugar. Stir until creamy, then set aside for 10 minutes.

2. Make a hole in the middle of the dry ingredients and pour in the yeast mixture. Add 2 cups of water and the oil.

3. Using a wooden spoon, mix to a soft dough. Add more water if needed—just how much depends on the type of flour. .

4. Tip out onto a lightly floured bench top and knead for 10 minutes, or until the dough is smooth and no longer sticky

5. Rub it lightly all over with oil and place in a large bowl in a warm place, covered with plastic wrap and a tea towel. Leave 1–2 hours or until dough has doubled in size—how long it takes depends on how warm the air is.

6. Preheat oven to 220°C (200°C fan-forced/410°F/Gas mark 6–7).

7. Knock the dough back firmly with your knuckles (punch it down), then turn out of the bowl and knead again for a few minutes on a lightly floured bench top.

8. Divide dough into pieces to fit inside your flowerpots. Fill pots to two-thirds full for a full top, or half fill for a lower top. Cover with plastic wrap and leave in a warm place for 40 minutes or until the dough has risen.

9. Brush tops with water, sprinkle with poppy, sesame or sunflower seeds and bake in oven for 40–45 minutes or until well risen and brown. Tip out while warm onto a wire rack.

Naughty but Nice Breakfast Fruit Bread

This is easy to make and a lovely one to do for mum on Mother's Day. You can use butter and a little honey instead of the ricotta if you prefer.

Preparation time: 10 minutes
Cooking time: 5–10 minutes
Serves: 2

equipment

Grill
Measuring cups and spoons
Small bowl
Fork or whisk
Juice squeezer
Small knife
Egg slicer

ingredients

2 slices good quality fruit bread
½ cup (125g/4oz) fresh ricotta, drained of any liquid
1 tablespoon brown sugar or honey
1 tablespoon freshly squeezed orange juice
Cinnamon sugar (2 tablespoons caster sugar mixed with ¼ teaspoon cinnamon)
1 banana, peach, mango 'cheek' or handful of strawberries

Tip: If you are using mangoes, slice off the cheeks and carefully peel away the skin, then slice the flesh. If you are using strawberries, wash them, cut off the green hulls and slice them lengthways.

method

1. Preheat grill to medium–high.
2. Put the ricotta in a small bowl and whisk with a fork until smooth. Add sugar (or honey) and orange juice. Stir well to combine.
3. Slice the fruit bread and toast it on one side.
4. Spread the ricotta mixture over the untoasted sides and top generously with sliced banana or other fruit. Sprinkle cinnamon sugar over the top.
5. Place under the grill and grill for 2–3 minutes or until sugar begins to caramelise. Use an egg slicer to remove the toasts from under the grill—be careful as the grill is very hot. Place them on a board and cut into halves. Serve immediately.

Buttermilk Pancakes

Preparation time: 10 minutes
Resting time: 15–20 minutes
Cooking time: 20 minutes
Makes: 12x12cm (5x5inches) pancakes
Serves: 4–6

"Mix a pancake,
Stir a pancake,
Pop it in the pan.
Fry the pancake,
Toss the pancake,
Catch it if you can!"
~ Christina Rossetti

equipment

Measuring cups and spoons
Food processor
Sifter
Medium jug
Medium non-stick frying pan
Spatula
Egg slicer

ingredients

2 cups (500ml/16fl oz)
   buttermilk
2 free range or organic eggs
2 tablespoons vegetable oil
1 ⅓ cups (200g) plain flour
2 tablespoons caster sugar
2 teaspoons baking powder
1 teaspoon bicarbonate of soda
1 teaspoon salt
Cooking oil spray

to serve

Maple or golden syrup
Knob of butter
Mixed berries, vanilla yoghurt
   and icing sugar

method

1. Put the buttermilk, eggs and oil into the bowl of a food processor or blender. Process until well combined.

2. Sift together the dry ingredients onto a piece of greaseproof paper and add to the buttermilk mixture. Process 1–2 minutes or until well combined. Scrape down the sides with a spatula and process for a few more seconds. Pour into a jug. Cover with plastic wrap and set aside for 15–20 minutes.

3. Lightly spray frying pan with cooking oil spray and place over moderate heat until hot. Pour in some of the batter, smoothing out with the spatula or back of a spoon. Make the pancakes about 12cm in diameter. Cook until small bubbles form on top, flip over and cook until golden on the other side.

4. Serve in a stack of 2–3 pancakes topped with a knob of butter and drizzle with maple syrup or golden syrup. Or serve with mixed berries, dusted with icing sugar and vanilla yoghurt.

Fresh Fruit Salad with Yoghurt

This is a basic fruit salad to which you can add your choice of fruits in season eg. mangoes in summer, pears in autumn. If you are using banana, add it just before you serve the salad so it doesn't go mushy and brown.

Preparation time: 20–25 minutes
Serves: 4–6

equipment

Kitchen knife
Vegetable peeler
Chopping board
Measuring spoons
Medium bowl

ingredients

2 oranges, peeled and cut in
   2cm (¾inch) pieces
1 apple, peeled and chopped in
   2cm (¾inch) pieces
1 pear, peeled and chopped in
   2cm (¾inch) pieces
¼ small sweet pineapple,
   peeled and chopped
1 punnet strawberries, washed,
   hulled and quartered
100g (3½oz) blueberries
100g (3½oz) seedless grapes
1 banana, peeled and sliced

fruit syrup

Juice of ½ orange
Juice of ½ lemon
3 passionfruit, pulp only
1 tablespoon caster sugar
Garnish: fresh small mint leaves

method

1. Combine all the fruit for the salad in a medium bowl and toss well to combine.
2. For the syrup: combine orange and lemon juice, passionfruit pulp and sugar in a small bowl. Stir well until sugar dissolves then pour over fruit. Garnish with mint leaves.
3. Serve with your favourite yoghurt or over your favourite muesli.

'Who wants breakfast?
Who wants tea?
Who wants everything just like me?
Honey for breakfast
Honey for tea
Honey for you
Honey for me.'

~ Traditional Nursery Rhyme

snacks

'Alice: I've had nothing yet, so I can't take more.
The Mad Hatter: You mean you can't take less; it's very easy to take more than nothing.'

~ *Alice in Wonderland* by Lewis Carroll

Isobel's Dried Fruit & Nut Slice

This delicious muesli-like slice is a good one for the school lunch box or for a snack. Hard to resist!

Preparation time: 20 minutes
Cooking time: 35–40 minutes
Makes 24 x 5cm (2inch) squares.

equipment

Medium mixing bowl
Sifter
Heatproof bowl
Saucepan
Wooden spoon
Measuring cups and spoons
Kitchen knife
Chopping board
Slice or slab tin
(20x30cm/8x12inch)

ingredients

1½ cups mixed nuts
(pistachios, pecans,
macadamias), roughly
chopped
1 cup (125g) dried apricots,
diced
1 cup (150g) sultanas
⅓ cup (50g) plain flour
1½ cups flaked or shredded
coconut
300g (10oz) white chocolate,
chopped
½ cup honey

Tip: If you lightly toast the nuts beforehand and leave them to cool, the flavour will be better.

method

1. Preheat oven to 160°C (140°C fan-forced/325°F/gas mark 3). Line a slab tin with non-stick baking paper.
2. In a bowl, combine the mixed nuts, apricots and sultanas. Sift the flour over the top. Add the coconut and combine well.
3. Place the chocolate and honey in a heatproof bowl and melt over simmering water. Pour over fruit and nut mixture and mix well to combine. It will be very sticky and you may need to use your hands to bring the mixture together.
4. Spoon into tin and press down hard to even out (if you dip your hand in milk, this will make it easier).
5. Bake 35–40 minutes until golden on top.
6. Remove from oven, mark into squares and leave to cool. Cut into squares and store in a screw-top jar.

Wendy's Sausage Rolls

These are easy to make, and even easier to eat!

Cooking time: 30–35 minutes
Makes 8 large or 20 small

equipment

Baking tray
Baking paper
Medium mixing bowl
Wooden spoon
Kitchen knife
Small bowl
Pastry brush

ingredients

500g (1lb) beef sausage mince
2 free range or organic eggs,
   beaten
1 medium onion, peeled and
   finely chopped
1 teaspoon thyme
½ cup seasoning mix
¼ cup beef stock
2 sheets frozen puff pastry,
   partially thawed

Egg wash
1 egg beaten with 2 teaspoons
   water

Two little sausages frying in a pan,
One went sizzle
And the other went bang!

-Far Out, Brussel Sprout! (page 91)

method

1. Preheat oven to 200°C (180°C fan-forced/400°F/gas mark 4). Line a baking tray with baking paper.
2. In a medium bowl, combine all the ingredients except the pastry. Mix together with a wooden spoon—or use your hands.
3. Divide mixture into four. Roll each one out into a sausage shape, making them the same length as the pastry sheets.
4. Cut each sheet of pastry in half. Place filling on pastry, about 3cm from edge. Brush edges of pastry with water. Fold pastry over and press to seal, with seam on bottom. Repeat with rest of pastry and filling.
5. Place on lined trays. Brush tops with egg wash. Bake for 30–35 minutes, swapping the trays around once, until the pastry is golden and the filling is cooked.
6. Remove from oven and cut each roll into 5 pieces (or 2 pieces for larger rolls). Serve with tomato sauce.

Anzac Choc Pops

Here's a twist on the traditional Anzac biscuit which I'm sure you'll really like.

Preparation time: 15 minutes
Cooking time: 20 minutes
Makes 20 biscuits

equipment

Measuring cups and spoons
Mixing bowl
Wooden spoon
Small saucepan
Baking trays
Baking paper
20 paddle pop sticks

ingredients

125g (4oz) butter
1 tablespoon golden syrup
2 tablespoons boiling water
1 teaspoon bi-carbonate soda
1 cup (200g) sugar
1 cup (150g) plain flour
1 cup (150g) rolled oats
1 cup (90g) desiccated coconut
2–3 tablespoons choc chips
Mini M&Ms to decorate

method

1. Preheat oven to 170°C (150°C fan-forced/300°F/Gas mark 2). Grease a couple of baking trays or line them with baking paper.
2. Combine the dry ingredients in a mixing bowl and toss to combine.
3. Melt the butter in a small saucepan. Add syrup and water and stir to dissolve. Remove pan from heat and add the bi-carbonate soda—it will froth up quickly so be careful.
3. Pour the butter mixture over the dry ingredients and mix well to combine. Stir in the choc chips.
4. Place rounded teaspoons of the mixture, about 5cm apart, on a greased baking tray, flattening them slightly. Insert a paddle pop stick into the base of each biscuit. Press mini M&Ms into the tops. Bake for about 18–20 minutes.

Mini carrot and currant muffins

Preparation time: 15–20 minutes
Cooking time: 15 minutes
Makes 36

equipment

Measuring cups and spoons
Grater
Sifter
2 medium mixing bowls
Wooden spoon
Mini muffin tins
Cake rack

ingredients

Cooking oil spray
1 cup (150g/4¾oz) plain flour
1 teaspoon bi-carbonate of soda
1 teaspoon cinnamon
¼ teaspoon salt
⅔ cup (60g/2 oz) oat bran
2 free range or organic eggs
¾ cup (125g/4oz) brown sugar
2 tablespoons vegetable oil
1 teaspoon vanilla extract
1 small carrot (75g/3oz), grated
⅓ cup (60g/2oz) currants
Icing sugar, for dusting

method

1. Preheat oven to 180°C (160°C fan-forced/350°F/gas mark 4). Lightly spray mini muffin tins with cooking oil spray.
2. In a mixing bowl, sift the flour together with the bi-carbonate of soda, cinnamon and salt and stir through the oat bran.
3. In another bowl, beat the eggs together with the sugar. When light and fluffy, whisk in the oil and vanilla. Stir in grated carrot and currants.
4. Make a hole in centre of flour mixture and tip in the egg mixture. Using a wooden spoon, stir to combine until just moist. Spoon batter into mini muffin tins.
5. Bake for 15 minutes or until golden and firm to the touch—or until a skewer inserted in the middle comes out clean. Turn out onto a cake rack to cool. Dust lightly with icing sugar.

Sweet Lamb Patties

These sweet fragrant meatballs are terrific served in a pide pocket or small hamburger bun or dinner roll, topped with hommus and mixed salad.

Preparation time: 15 minutes
Cooking time: 10 minutes
Makes 10 (or 20 mini patties)

equipment

Chopping board
Kitchen knife
Medium mixing bowl and small
  bowl
Small tray
Medium frying pan

ingredients

2 tablespoons olive oil
1 medium onion, finely chopped
500g (1lb) lamb mince
1 teaspoon cinnamon
1 tablespoon freshly chopped
  mint leaves (optional)
1 tablespoon pine nuts
1 small egg, beaten with ½
  teaspoon salt and freshly
  ground pepper

method

1. Heat oil in a frypan and fry the onion until soft. Remove and cool.
2. Combine remaining ingredients in a medium mixing bowl, add the cooked onion and, using your hands, form into 10 small patties (about 7cm/2¾inches in diameter). Place them on a small tray, cover and refrigerate for 20 minutes.
3. Using the same frying pan, cook the meatballs in two batches until they are evenly brown all over and cooked through, about 4–5 minutes on each side.

Christmas Bruschetta (Italian Toasts)

Preparation time: 15–20 minutes
Makes 12–18

equipment

Baking tray
Kitchen knife
Bread knife
Chopping board

Tip: A little crumbled fetta sprinkled over the top is a delicious addition.

ingredients

1 French bread stick (or baguette), sliced diagonally into 12–18 pieces
1 clove garlic, halved
3 ripe medium red and yellow tomatoes, washed and diced
1 small Spanish onion, peeled and finely diced
Sea salt
Freshly ground black pepper
3–4 tablespoons olive oil
3–4 tablespoons fresh basil, chopped

method

1. Preheat oven to 180°C (160°C fan-forced/400°F/Gas mark 6).
2. Place bread slices on a baking tray. Toast the bread in oven until just golden.
3. When cool, rub each slice with the half clove of garlic. Set aside.
4. Put tomatoes in a bowl. Add the onion. Season with salt and pepper. Stir through the oil and basil. Taste and add more seasoning, oil or basil if required. Cover and refrigerate until 10–15 minutes before serving.
5. Using a teaspoon, top each bruschetta with some of the tomato mixture. This is best served within an hour of topping—otherwise, the toast will become soggy.

snacks

Easy Peasy Scones

These are delicious served with butter or whipped cream and raspberry jam. For soft scones, wrap in a clean tea towel for ten minutes as soon as they come out of the oven. For crusty scones, cool on a wire rack.

Preparation time: 15 minutes
Cooking time: 16–18 minutes
Makes 10 scones

equipment

Measuring cups and spoons
Mixing bowl
Baking trays
Baking paper
5–6cm (2–2½inch) scone
  cutter or glass
Pastry brush

ingredients

2½ cups (375g/12oz) self-
  raising flour
½ teaspoon salt
½ cup (115g/3¾oz) caster
  sugar
300ml (10fl oz) pouring cream
50–75ml (2–3fl oz) water
Milk, for brushing tops

method

1. Preheat oven to 230°C (210°C fan-forced/500°F/Gas mark 9). Line a baking tray with baking paper.
2. Sift the flour, salt and sugar into a mixing bowl. Make a well in the centre and pour in the cream and water. Mix all ingredients together to make a soft but not sticky dough.
3. Knead lightly on a floured bench top and pat out to 2cm (1 inch) thickness. Be careful not to overwork the dough. Turn over so that smooth side is on top.
4. With a scone cutter or glass dipped in flour, cut into 5cm (2inch) rounds and place close together on the baking tray — this helps them to support each other as they rise, and to retain their moisture.
5. Brush tops with milk and bake for 15–18 minutes or until well risen and golden.

Variations: For fruit scones, stir through 2 x 40g (1oz) mini sultana and apricot or sultana and apple packs or ½ cup sultanas and a little mixed spice.

It's going, it's going...
It's scone.

sandwiches

Use your imagination when it comes to spreads on bread and try different ones such as mashed avocado, hommus, lite cream cheese or mayonnaise.

Try to replace the standard sandwich bread with something similar but more exciting like a tortilla, mountain bread, a wrap, or pita-pocket bread. You can find whole-wheat bagels and a variety of healthy wraps at most grocery stores.

Or try a sandwich wand—use metal or bamboo skewers to thread on alternate cubes of cheddar or firm fetta cheese with cubes of ham, cooked turkey or chicken breast, and vegies such as cherry tomatoes and button mushrooms.

Peter's Chicken Sandwiches

Preparation time: 25 minutes
Makes 6 whole sandwiches, or 24 quarters.

equipment

Breadboard
Mixing bowl
Bread knife, for cutting the
  sandwiches

Tip: For luxurious chicken sandwiches, add 2 tablespoons sour cream and 2 tablespoons chopped fresh pistachios. For egg sandwiches, substitute 3–4 boiled, peeled and chopped eggs for the chicken.

ingredients

300g (9½oz) cooked chicken,
  diced
½ cup (125ml/4fl oz)
  mayonnaise
1 tablespoon freshly chopped
  flat leaf parsley
1 tablespoon finely chopped
  chives
1 stick celery, diced
Salt and pepper, to taste
Softened butter
12 slices white and/or
  wholemeal bread

method

1. Combine the chicken, mayonnaise, herbs and celery in a bowl. Mix well and season to taste.
2. Butter the bread, Spread the filling over six slices, top with remaining six slices, trim the crusts and cut into quarters. Ask an adult to help with cutting the bread.

BLAT!

These bacon, lettuce, avocado and tomato toasted sandwiches are great to make when you're starving and need a quick fix.

Preparation time: 15 minutes
Cooking time: 5 minutes
Makes 4 sandwiches

equipment

Breadboard
Mixing bowl
Bread knife, for cutting the
    sandwiches

ingredients

4 x 10cm (4inch) pieces Turkish
    bread, sliced in half
2 ripe avocadoes, cut in half,
    seed removed
2–3 medium tomatoes
Salt and freshly cracked black
    pepper
8 slices bacon, cooked until
    crisp
8 lettuce leaves (oak leaf or
    butter lettuce)

method

1. Toast the bread. Spread each slice with avocado.
2. Take four slices and top each one with 2 or 3 slices of tomato. Season with salt and pepper. Top with crispy slices of warm bacon and lettuce leaves.
3. Cover with the remaining slices of toast, press together gently and serve immediately.

Steak Sandwich

If you make these juicy toasted sandwiches for Dad on Sunday afternoon when he's watching football, I bet you'll be in his good books all week. Best eaten while the steaks are still hot and juicy.

Preparation time:15 minutes
Cooking time: 10 minutes
Makes 4 sandwiches.

equipment

Breadboard
Mixing bowl
Bread knife, for cutting the
  sandwiches
Char-grill pan

ingredients

Cooking oil spray
4 x 150g (5oz) pieces best
  quality steak (rump, scotch
  fillet), about 1cm(½inch) thick
4 rolls, split in half lengthwise
Softened butter
Dijonnaise or mayonnaise
Iceberg lettuce leaves, washed
  and dried
2 ripe tomatoes, sliced
½ red onion, thinly sliced
  (optional) or cheese slices
Salt and cracked pepper
Tomato or barbecue sauce
  (optional)

method

1. Trim steaks of fat. Spray with oil spray if you are using a char-grill pan.
2. Heat the char-grill pan (or grill) and cook the steaks for 2–3 minutes on each side.
3. Remove from heat when cooked to your liking and season with salt and pepper. Cover with foil to keep warm
3. Toast the insides of the rolls under the grill. Watch carefully to make sure they don't burn. Spread each side with dijonnaise or mayonnaise.
4. Top with the cooked steaks then with a few tomato slices, some red onion rings or a cheese slice (if using) and some lettuce leaves. Drizzle with tomato or barbecue sauce. Ask an adult to help you cut it in half for easier eating.

Ice cream Sandwiches

Makes 4

equipment

Lamington or slab tin
Baking paper
Metal spoon
Small tray

ingredients

1 tub softened ice cream, (use
  your favourite flavour)
8x2.2g ($^1/_8$oz) natural wafers
  (9.5x5.5cm/4x2½inch)
hundreds and thousands, or
  chocolate sprinkles

method

1. Line a lamington or slab tin with baking paper. Spread the ice cream over the tin and smooth the top with a spoon dipped in hot water. It should be about 5cm (2inches) thick. Return to freezer to harden.

2. Remove from freezer and tip out onto another sheet of baking paper on the benchrop. Cut out pieces to fit the wafers. Place a wafer on top and bottom and smooth out the sides.

3. Place ice cream sandwiches on a small tray and freeze until firm. If you like, you can dip the sides of the ice cream sandwich in hundreds and thousands or chocolate sprinkles before freezing.

I scream
You scream
We all scream
For ice cream.

And I bet you'll scream if you miss out on one of these!

starters

'Eat away, chew away, munch and bolt
and guzzle, Never leave the table
till you're full up to the muzzle.'

- The Magic Pudding, by Norman Lindsay

Potato and Leek Soup

This is a really flavoursome soup which the whole family will love. To really impress your parents, puree the soup with 150ml (5fl oz) fresh cream to make a French classic known as Vichyssoise which is delicious hot or cold. A good one to take on a picnic in a thermos or airtight container!

Preparation time: 20 minutes
Cooking time: 40 minutes
Serves 4–6

equipment

Kitchen knife or turbo whiz
Measuring cups and spoons
Chopping board
Kitchen knife
Medium large saucepan
Soup ladle
Food processor or blender

ingredients

1 tablespoon vegetable oil
30g (1oz) butter
1 onion, peeled and chopped
1 large leek, white part only, sliced
4 medium potatoes (600–700g/19–22oz), peeled and sliced
Chicken stock to cover, approx 750ml (26fl oz)
Salt to taste

garnish:

Fresh cream (optional)
Small bunch freshly chopped dill or chives

Tip: This soup is very versatile because you can substitute other vegetables (such as pumpkin, kumara, carrots, broccoli or zucchini) for the potatoes—but make sure to use one potato to act as a thickener.

method

1. Heat the oil and butter in medium pan. Add the onion and cook gently for 2–3 minutes. Add the leek, cover with a lid, and leave to sweat until leek is soft, about 10 minutes.
2. Add the potatoes, cover with chicken stock and simmer gently until potatoes are soft, about 20–30 minutes.
3. Remove from stove and puree in a food processor or blender. Use a ladle to transfer soup into food processor and do it in 2–3 batches. Be very careful as the soup is hot. Ask an adult for help with this. Season to taste. Can be thinned with more chicken stock or water, if required. Serve immediately, garnished with freshly chopped dill or chives and a swirl of cream.

Chicken Noodle Soup

In our household, this is known as 'get-better-soon' soup. Make sure you use a good chicken stock so that the soup is really flavoursome. If you prefer, substitute wontons or mini dim sims for the noodles and use vegies of your choice.

Preparation time: 15 minutes
Cooking time: 10–15 minutes
Serves: 4–6

equipment

Measuring cups and spoons
Chopping board
Medium bowl
Strainer
Vegetable peeler
Medium saucepan
Kitchen knife

Tip: You'll find pre-cut chicken breast strips in the refrigerated section of your supermarket. A handful of snow peas (trimmed and halved), sugar snaps or bean sprouts (topped and tailed) are a nice addition.

ingredients

200g (6½oz) fresh Singapore or thin egg noodles, cut with scissors
5–6 cups (1¼–1½L/44fl oz) chicken stock
1 carrot, peeled, halved lengthways and sliced
200g chicken breast, cut into 1cm(¼inch) strips)
1 fresh cob of corn (approx 125g/4oz), kernels removed
1 stalk celery, sliced
1–2 tablespoons soy sauce
Salt, to taste

garnish:

2 spring onions, sliced thinly on the diagonal (optional)
Few drops of sesame oil (optional)

method

1. Place noodles in a medium heatproof bowl, cover with boiling water and leave to stand for 2–3 minutes. Drain and set aside.
2. Heat the chicken stock in a medium saucepan. While stock simmers, add the carrots and cook 2–3 minutes.
3. Add the chicken breast strips and corn kernels and cook for 1 minute. Add celery, soy sauce and noodles. Simmer very gently for 2–3 minutes or until chicken is cooked—don't let it boil. Season to taste and simmer for 30 seconds.
4. Ladle into warm serving bowls and top with sliced green onions and a few drops of sesame oil, if using.

Evi's Vegetable Soup

This delicious vegetable soup comes from the island of Lesbos in Greece. It's easy to make—just make sure to cut all the vegetables the same size so they cook evenly.

Preparation time: 20 minutes
Cooking time: 40 minutes
Serves: 4–6

equipment

Kitchen knife or turbo wiz
Measuring cups and spoons
Chopping board
Medium saucepan
Vegetable peeler
Kitchen knife
Food processor or blender

ingredients

1 leek, white part only, sliced and washed
1 medium onion, peeled and chopped
2 medium-small potatoes, peeled and chopped
¼ butternut pumpkin, peeled and chopped
1 zucchini, washed and sliced
1 celery stalk, chopped
2 small carrots, peeled and chopped
1 clove garlic, finely chopped
1 small red chilli, deseeded (optional)
Chicken stock to cover
Salt and cracked black pepper
15g (½oz) butter

method

1. Put all the vegetables in a medium saucepan. Cover with chicken stock and bring to the boil.
2. Turn down heat and simmer gently, covered, until vegetables are soft. Season with salt and pepper and add the butter, cook another minute.
3. Remove from heat. Puree the vegetables in a blender or food processor in batches. Use a soup ladle to transfer the soup into bowls.

Lettuce cups, Chinese-style

You've probably tried this Chinese dish (called Sang Choy Bao). It's traditionally enjoyed as finger food and wrapped in a lettuce leaf

Preparation time: 20 minutes
Cooking time: 10 minutes
Serves: 6–8

equipment

Measuring cups and spoons
Chopping board
Kitchen knife
Wok or large frying pan
Large bowl
Ice
Scissors

Tip: Look for 'sweetheart' lettuces at your greengrocer or supermarket. They are mini icebergs and easier to separate into leaves.

ingredients

2 teaspoons vegetable oil
300g (9½oz) lean pork mince (or chicken, if you prefer)
¼ teaspoon salt
¼ teaspoon sugar
1 small white onion, peeled and finely chopped
1 teaspoon freshly grated ginger
2 stalks celery, finely chopped
1 small Lebanese cucumber, seeded, halved lengthways and finely chopped
2 tablespoons chicken stock
1 tablespoon soy sauce or oyster sauce
1 teaspoon toasted sesame oil
2 teaspoons cornflour, mixed with 1 tablespoon water
1 small iceberg or butter lettuce, washed, with 8 leaves separated (keep in iced water until ready to serve)

method

1. In a frypan or wok, heat the oil over low heat and add the pork with the sugar and salt. Stir-fry until the meat has browned.
2. Add onion, ginger, celery and cucumber. Stir-fry for a minute. Add chicken stock, soy sauce and sesame oil and cook for about a minute. Add cornflour mixture, cook for a further minute, stirring while the sauce thickens. Remove from heat and place in a serving bowl.
3. Remove lettuce leaves from the iced water and shake off any water. Cut with scissors into neat cup shapes. Spoon meat into lettuce leaves and roll into a neat parcel.

Hommus Dip

This is an easy, nutritious dip and a good one for the school lunchbox. Use tinned chickpeas, but drain and rinse them well under cold running water. Excellent with BBQ lamb skewers, spinach or beetroot-flavoured corn chips or toasted wholemeal pide.

Preparation time: 15 minutes
Makes 2½ cups

equipment

Measuring cups and spoons
Chopping board
Food processor or blender
Garlic crusher

ingredients

2 x 410g (13oz) cans chickpeas,
   drained and rinsed
¼ cup olive oil
¼ cup tahini (well-stirred)
2 cloves garlic, crushed
½ teaspoon salt
1–2 tablespoons lemon juice
½ cup cold water
Ground cumin or paprika, to
   sprinkle on top

method

1. Place the chickpeas, oil, tahini, garlic, salt and lemon juice in a food processor and process until combined.
2. With motor running, pour in the water and continue processing until smooth (this helps to make it creamy).
3. Serve sprinkled with a little cumin or paprika.

> *Tip: For the toasted wholemeal pide, cut the pide in half, then cut into triangles. Place on a baking tray, spray each side lightly with olive oil spray and cook in a moderate oven until crispy, about 10–15 minutes*

Angela's Avocado Dip

This lovely creamy dip is a terrific alternative to the better known guacamole. Good as a dip with rainbow vegetable sticks—or serve it with lamb kebabs or grilled cutlets.

Preparation time: 10 minutes

equipment

Measuring cups and spoons
Chopping board
Food processor or blender

Tip: To make rainbow vegetable sticks, peel carrots, cut in half lengthways then slice into matchsticks. Cut celery and capsicum into matchsticks of the same length.

ingredients

1 large avocado, seeded, peeled and mashed
1 cup (250ml/8fl oz) creamy natural yoghurt
½ clove garlic, finely chopped (optional)
2 tablespoons fresh basil, chopped
2 tablespoons fresh mint, chopped
1 small Lebanese cucumber, seeded and finely diced
Salt and freshly cracked pepper
Juice of ½ lemon

method

1. Combine all the ingredients in a bowl, mix well.
2. Taste for seasoning and add more herbs, lemon juice or salt and pepper to suit your taste.

salads and sides

'Pardon me for being rude
It was not me
It was my food.
It got so lonely down below
It just came up
To say "Hullo".'

~ Unreal, Banana Peel! (p5)

Edible Flower Farm Salad

This salad is almost too beautiful to eat!

Preparation time: 10–15 minutes
Serves: 4 as a side salad or entrée

equipment

Salad spinner
Salad bowl
Measuring spoons

ingredients

Mixture of baby salad leaves
(baby Cos, baby red and
green oakleaf, coral lettuce,
butter lettuce, rocket, tender
curly endive, chervil and
mizuna)
Mixture of edible flower petals
(nasturtiums, borage, Heart's
ease, violets, pansies,
geraniums, chrysanthemums,
herb blossoms)

method

1. Wash and dry the leaves and flower petals carefully. Toss together gently in a salad bowl.
2. Make a dressing with three parts light olive oil and one part white balsamic vinegar.

The Vegie Garden Salad with Classic Vinagrette Dressing

This is a basic mixed salad which you can serve on its own or to accompany a main dish. You can use whatever vegetables you like in this salad, including cauliflower or broccoli florets, avocado, fennel and bean sprouts – mix and match according to your tastes.

Preparation time: 15–20 minutes
Serves: 4 as a side salad or entrée

equipment

Salad spinner
Salad bowl
Measuring spoons
Kitchen knife
Vegetable peeler
Chopping board

Tip: You can double or triple the dressing ingredients depending on how much you want to use. The dressing will keep for up to 2 weeks, refrigerated in an airtight container.

ingredients

4 cups (about 200g/6½oz) mixed lettuce leaves
1 carrot, peeled and sliced into matchsticks
1 lebanese cucumber, deseeded and cut into matchsticks
2 celery stalks, sliced into matchsticks
2 tomatoes, cut into eight wedges each
1 green or red capsicum, cut into strips
Freshly chopped parsley, mint or basil

dressing

3 tablespoons extra virgin olive oil
1 tablespoon vinegar (red wine, white wine or white balsamic)
1 small clove garlic, crushed
½ teaspoon salt
2 teaspoons Dijon mustard
½ teaspoon sugar (optional)
Freshly ground black pepper

method

1. Wash and dry the lettuce leaves—it's easy if you do this in a salad spinner. Pile the leaves into a salad bowl and mix with remaining ingredients. Toss gently to combine.
2. To make the dressing, put all the dressing ingredients in a screw-top jar and shake until thick and well combined.
3. Drizzle dressing over the salad, be careful not to overdress the salad or it will become soggy.

Pesto Pasta Salad with Cherry Tomatoes

This makes a delicious lunch or main course and is a good one for the lunchbox.

Preparation time: 10–15 minutes
Cooking time: 12 minutes
Serves: 6–8

equipment

Large saucepan
Small pan
Colander or strainer
Kitchen knife
Chopping board
Grater

ingredients

500g (1lb) short pasta (spirals are best)
6 chicken tenderloins (about 400g/13oz)
salt and freshly cracked pepper
1 tablespoon olive oil
1 punnet cherry or grape tomatoes, washed and halved
¾ cup macadamia basil pesto (see page 97)
¾ cup pouring cream, heated in a small pan
60g (2oz) parmesan cheese, shaved or grated

Tip: For variety, use interesting pasta shapes (try kangaroos or koala-shapes when overseas relatives are visiting!). Or, try the following additions:
• Sliced celery
• Pitted small black olives
• Toasted macadamia pieces
• Roasted red or yellow capsicum strips.

method

1. Cook pasta in a large saucepan of boiling, salted water, following packet directions, until just tender (about 8–10 minutes). Drain. Return to saucepan.
2. Meanwhile, season the tenderloins with salt and pepper. Heat the oil in a frying pan and cook the chicken until golden, about 3–4 minutes on each side. Remove from heat, cover with a lid and keep warm. Cut into bite-size pieces when cool enough to handle.
3. Toss the tomatoes in the pan juices, tossing until just warmed through.
2. Mix the pesto with the cream in the pasta pan and stir well to combine over low heat. Add the drained pasta, cooked chicken and tomatoes and toss well. Season to taste and serve with shaved or grated parmesan.
5. If not using immediately store in a plastic container in the refrigerator.

Macaroni and Vegetable Cheese Bake

This is a terrific stand-by as it keeps well. If you don't like peas or corn, use vegetables you like (such as cooked broccoli florets or sliced zucchini or roasted capsicum strips). Crispy diced bacon or diced ham is also a yummy addition. Remember to prepare the topping of your choice in advance.

Preparation time: 15 minutes
Cooking time: 35 minutes
Serves: 8 as a side dish

equipment

Saucepan
1½L (48fl oz) ovenproof baking
   dish

ingredients

⅔ cup (100g/3oz) dried
   macaroni
200g (6oz) fresh peas, shelled
   (about ¾ cup)
1 x 225g (6½oz) cob of corn,
   kernels only (about ¾ cup)
1 quantity white sauce (see
   page 96)
1 cup grated cheese (tasty or Swiss)
Salt and pepper

Yankee Doodle went to town
A riding on a pony
He stuck a feather in his hat
And called it macaroni

ingredients continued

topping 1

½ cup grated mozzarella cheese

2 tablespoons cornflakes, crushed

2 tablespoons snipped chives

1 teaspoon dried oregano (optional)

To make this topping, combine all the ingredients in a bowl.

topping 2

1 tablespoon olive oil

1–2 cloves garlic, crushed

2 rashers bacon, rind removed and diced

¾ cup fresh breadcrumbs

2 tablespoons snipped chives

1 teaspoon dried oregano (optional)

To make this topping, heat the oil in a medium frying pan, add the garlic and cook for one minute. Add the bacon and cook until it turns crispy. Stir through the breadcrumbs, chives and oregano, mixing well to combine.

method

1. Preheat oven to 180ºC (160ºC fan-forced/350ºF/Gas mark 4).
2. Cook the macaroni in a large saucepan of rapidly boiling salted water for 7 minutes. Add the peas and corn kernels and cook another 2–3 minutes or until macaroni and vegetables are tender. Drain and run under cold water. Set aside.
3. Stir the white sauce through the reserved macaroni and vegetables.
4. Spoon macaroni into an ovenproof dish or into four small ovenproof bowls. Sprinkle with cheese and the topping of your choice.
5. Place in moderate oven and bake for 20 minutes until hot and golden on top.

Cauliflower Cheese

My kids always loved this dish. You can use broccoli—or mix the cauliflower and broccoli together. Prepare the cauliflower/broccoli by cutting it into florets and slit the stem with a small knife to help it steam evenly.

Preparation time: 10–15 minutes
Cooking time: 15–20 minutes
Serves: 4 as a side dish

equipment

Chopping board
Kitchen knife
Steamer or microwave-proof
  bowl
Medium saucepan
Wooden bowl
1 litre (32fl oz) ovenproof dish

ingredients

300g (10oz) cauliflower florets
1 quantity white sauce
  (see page 96)
½ cup grated tasty cheese
¼ cup grated fresh parmesan
  cheese
Salt and pepper
Pinch of nutmeg or dried thyme
  (optional)

topping

1 tablespoon cornflake crumbs
1 tablespoon grated parmesan

method

1. Steam the cauliflower florets (or cook in the microwave) until tender.
2. Preheat grill to medium high.
3. Place cauliflower florets in ovenproof dish. Pour the white sauce, with cheese added, over the top.
4. Combine the cornflake crumbs and parmesan cheese and sprinkle over the top. Place under the grill about 10cm (4inches) from the heat for five minutes or until golden on top.

salads and sides

White Sauce

Makes 1½ cups.

equipment

Medium saucepan
Measuring cups and spoons
Wooden spoon
Sieve

ingredients

40g (1½oz) unsalted butter
3 tablespoons plain flour
1 teaspoon mustard powder
½ teaspoon paprika
1½–2 cups hot milk
Salt and white pepper

method

1. In a small-medium saucepan, melt the butter over low heat.
2. Remove pan from heat and stir in the flour, mustard and paprika to make a paste ('roux').
3. Return pan to heat and cook gently 1–2 minutes until paste bubbles. Remove from heat and stir in the hot milk.
4. Return to heat and stir constantly until sauce boils and thickens. Add salt and pepper to taste. If sauce is lumpy, push it through a sieve before proceeding.

Tip: For Cheese Sauce: add 1 – 1½ cups grated cheese (such as tasty cheddar, parmesan, mozzarella or gruyere) to the sauce when hot. Stir well to combine. Use for macaroni cheese, cauliflower cheese, lasagne and moussaka. For a thinner sauce, add ½ cup hot milk.

Macadamia Pesto

Use this pesto to toss through pasta (spiral pasta, known as fusili, is best because it catches all the pesto, or try the egg pasta) or as a topping for pizza or bruschetta. It's also delicious stirred through soups or added to frittatas. The macadamias add a whole new dimension to the flavour.

Makes 1 ½ cups.
Preparation time: 15 minutes

equipment

Salad spinner
Measuring cups and spoons
Chopping board
Kitchen knife
Food processor or blender

ingredients

2 cups basil leaves, tightly packed
1 cup (150g (5oz) unsalted macadamias
3 cloves garlic, peeled
125ml (4fl oz) macadamia or olive oil
¾ cup (65g/2oz) freshly grated parmesan
½ teaspoon sea salt

method

1. Wash and dry the leaves thoroughly in a salad spinner.
2. Put leaves in a food processor or blender with the macadamias and garlic and process until well combined, adding a little of the oil if it's too dry. Scrape down sides and process again. Add the parmesan and salt, process again, then slowly drizzle in the oil, keeping the machine running. Process until smooth.
3. Scrape pesto into a tightly sealed jar or plastic container until ready to use—a film of macadamia or olive oil over the top will help to preserve it. Store in refrigerator.

main courses

'Mary had a little lamb,
Her brother had some chicken,
And so betwixt them both you see
They did some finger lickin'.'

~ All Right, Vegemite (p64)

Linden's Spag Bol

The longer you leave this to simmer on the stove, the better its flavour will be. It will also improve in flavour if left overnight and taste even better! My son, Linden, has always loved Spag Bol—he substitutes sweet chilli sauce for the tomato paste.

Preparation time: 20 minutes
Cooking time: 1 hour
Serves: 4–6

equipment

Measuring cups and spoons
Kitchen knife
Medium frying pan
Medium saucepan with lid
Wooden spoon
Slotted spoon
Simmer pad

ingredients

500g (1lb) beef mince
3 tablespoons light olive oil or
   vegetable oil
1 medium onion, peeled and
   chopped
1 stalk celery, strings peeled,
   and chopped
1 carrot, peeled and chopped
2–3 cloves garlic, peeled and
   finely chopped
Beef stock or water, approx
   2 cups (500ml/16fl oz) or
   enough to cover mince
1 teaspoon salt
Freshly ground pepper
1 x 410g (13oz) can peeled and
   diced tomatoes
1 teaspoon dried oregano
½ cup chopped fresh flat-leaf
   parsley
1 bay leaf (optional)
4 tablespoons tomato paste (or
   sweet chilli sauce)
500g (1lb) spaghetti

method

1. Heat 1 tablespoon of the oil in a frypan. Add half the meat and fry until brown and crumbly, stirring occasionally and breaking it up with a wooden spoon. Remove from pan to a plate and cover to keep warm. Repeat with the remaining meat.

2. Heat remaining oil in a frypan and fry the onion, celery, carrot and garlic until lightly brown (add a little water if needed). Return the meat to the pan and add remaining ingredients, except for the spaghetti. Bring to the boil, turn down heat to low, cover with a lid and simmer very gently for about 1 hour (or longer, if you have time). If you use a simmer pad, it will prevent the meat from cooking too quickly. Stir occasionally and add boiling water if it becomes dry.

3. Cook the spaghetti in plenty of rapidly boiling salted water for 7–8 minutes. Drain well before combining with the hot sauce. Serve with plenty of freshly grated parmesan.

Variations
• Add a small tin of mushrooms (in butter) or use fresh mushrooms (about 200g). These will need to be sliced and cooked gently in butter before adding to the meat and will add more flavour to the sauce.
• If you have an allergy to gluten, you can use this sauce with rice noodles or rice sticks (instead of spaghetti) for a satisfying and nutritious meal.
• Make Bolognese Jaffles with leftover Spag Bol in a jaffle or toasted sandwich maker.
• Or make lasagne with the meat mixture.

Tip: I like to give the sauce a whiz in the food processor to make it smoother, but that's optional.

Linden's Spag Bol

Chilli Con Carne Tacos

Chilli Con Carne Tacos

Once you've made the Chilli con carne, you can spoon it into individual cos or iceberg lettuce leaves for Chilli con Carne lettuce boats, or enclose it inside a burrito, or use it to make Nachos.

Preparation time: 20–25 minutes
Cooking time: 20–25 minutes
Makes 12 tacos

equipment

Measuring cups and spoons
Large frying pan or wok
Kitchen knife
Chopping board
Wooden spoon
Grater
Garlic crusher
Small bowls

ingredients

500g (1lb) beef or chicken mince
2–3 tablespoons vegetable oil, for frying
1 onion, peeled and chopped
½ green capsicum, cored, deseeded and chopped
1 stalk celery, diced
1 garlic clove, crushed
1 teaspoon cumin
1 teaspoon Mexican chilli powder
¾ cup tomato puree
1 x 400g(13oz) can kidney beans, rinsed and drained
12 taco shells
Salt and pepper

to serve

1 iceberg lettuce, washed and shredded
2 tomatoes, washed finely chopped
1 carrot, peeled and grated
1 cup grated tasty cheddar cheese
1 avocado, peeled and diced
Salsa or sour cream

method

1. Fry the mince in a frypan or wok with 1 tablespoon oil until brown and crumbly, stirring occasionally and breaking it up with a wooden spoon. Remove from pan and cover to keep warm.
2. Add 1–2 tablespoons oil to the pan, then add the onion, capsicum, celery and garlic and cook until onion begins to turn brown, stirring occasionally. Stir in the spices. Return mince to pan and season to taste with salt and pepper.
3. Add the tomato puree and kidney beans and mix well. Cover and cook gently for 10–15 minutes, mashing the mince and beans occasionally with a fork—add some water if mixture becomes too thick.
4. Heat taco shells in oven for five minutes and place on a serving platter.
5. To serve, place a little of the mixture on each taco shell then top with your favourite things: tomatoes, carrot, avocado, cheese, lettuce, salsa or sour cream.

For Nachos: tip a packet of plain corn chips over the base of an ovenproof dish, spoon over some of the Chilli Con Carne, top with home-made tomato sauce, sprinkle with grated tasty cheese and bake in a moderate oven (180°C/160°C fan-forced/300°F/Gas mark 4) for 10 minutes. Serve with Angela's Avocado Dip (see Snacks).

Pizzas

It's fun to make pizza from scratch because you can get your hands stuck into it—make sure your hands are really clean because they'll be doing plenty of work.

Preparation time: 15–20 minutes
Rising time: 1–2 hours
Cooking time: 15–20 minutes
Makes 3 large pizzas

equipment

Measuring cups and spoons
Kitchen knife
Large mixing bowl
Wooden spoon
Large chopping board
Plastic wrap
4 baking trays lined with baking paper
Oven mitts

ingredients

4 cups (600g/19oz) plain flour
2 teaspoons (1 sachet) dry yeast
2 teaspoons salt
1 teaspoon sugar
Approx. 1¼ cups warm water
1 tablespoon olive oil
'Sugo' sauce (see page 108)
Your favourite pizza topping
  (see opposite for suggestions)

method

1. Mix the flour, yeast, salt and sugar in a large bowl and make a well in the centre. Pour in the water and oil. Mix with a wooden spoon until most of the flour is incorporated, adding more water if needed, then use your hands to mix until a soft dough forms.
2. Turn the dough out onto the benchtop. Sprinkle with flour and knead for about 10 minutes or until smooth.
3. Transfer dough to a lightly greased bowl, brush the top with a little warm water, cover with plastic wrap and a tea towel set aside in a warm draught-free place until doubled in size— depending on the day, this can take between 1–2 hours (the warmer the weather, the quicker it will rise).

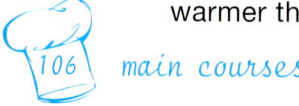

4. Preheat oven to 240°C (220°C fan-forced/500°F/Gas mark 9).
5. Punch the dough down and knead on a lightly floured benchtop for about 1 minute.
6. Divide dough into quarters and roll out each quarter on a lightly floured surface to about 30cm(12inch) diameter. Place on baking trays lined with baking paper.
7. Spread base with tomato 'sugo' sauce then top with a topping of your choice. Cook for 15–20 minutes or until crisp and golden.
8. Remove from the oven and top with freshly torn basil or rocket leaves.

Topping suggestions
- *Sliced mozzarella or bocconcini*
- *Crumbled fetta or goat cheese*
- *Grated parmesan and mozzarella cheese*
- *Strips of ham, salami or prosciutto*
- *Sliced mushrooms*
- *Halved black or green olives*
- *Diced bacon*
- *Roasted eggplant or red capsicum slices*
- *Char-grilled sliced zucchini*
- *Pineapple pieces, drained*
- *Teaspoonfuls of basil pesto*

Tip: You can wrap individual portions of dough in plastic wrap and freeze them for up to 3 months. Thaw in fridge overnight before using.

Mini Pizza Faces: stamp our rounds of dough with a 7.5cm (3inch) cutter, spread with sugo, sprinkle with a little cheese and cook in oven until golden and crusty around the edges. Remove and when cool enough to handle, make faces using sliced stuffed green olives for eyes; alfalfa sprouts for hair; thinly sliced button mushrooms for ears; and thin slices of halved tomatoes for mouths.

Tomato 'Sugo' Sauce

Preparation time: 10 minutes
Cooking time: 30 minutes

equipment

Measuring cups and spoons
Kitchen knife
Chopping board
Fork or potato masher
Medium saucepan
Simmer pad

ingredients

3–4 tablespoons extra virgin
  olive oil
2 garlic cloves, chopped finely
1 x 410g (13oz) can diced
  tomatoes
1 teaspoon dried oregano
  (optional)
¼ teaspoon sugar
Salt and pepper

method

1. Heat the oil in a pan, add garlic and cook over medium heat until soft.
2. Add the tomatoes, oregano and sugar. Mash tomatoes with a fork or potato masher. Leave to simmer gently on a simmer pad for 20–30 minutes. Season to taste.

Golden Roast Chicken

There can be nothing more delicious than a good, home-cooked roast chook. And you won't need any gravy for this one as the juices are really delicious.

Preparation time: 10 minutes
Standing time (marinade): 2–3 hours
Roasting time: 1 hour
Serves: 4

equipment

Paper towels
Measuring spoons
Small bowl
Roasting tray
Skewer
Oven mitts
Aluminium foil

ingredients

2 tablespoons olive oil
1 tablespoon ground cumin
1 teaspoon ground turmeric
1 large clove garlic, crushed
1 teaspoon salt
1 juicy lemon, washed well
1 x 1.4kg (2¾lb) chicken

method

1. In a small bowl, mix together all the ingredients except for the lemon and the chicken. Wipe chicken dry, trim excess fat. Rub marinade over the chicken, cover with plastic wrap and refrigerate for half an hour.

2. Preheat oven to 180°C (160°C fan-forced/350°F/Gas mark 4). Remove chicken from refrigerator and take off plastic wrap. Prick the lemon all over with a skewer and insert it inside the cavity of the chicken.

3. Place chicken on a rack in a baking dish and roast until just tender, about 1 hour.

4. Remove chicken from oven and cover with foil. Leave 10–15 minutes in a warm place before carving. Serve with the juices.

Lemon Potatoes

This is a great accompaniment to the Golden Roast Chicken. If you are making the chicken as well, sit the chicken on top of the potatoes in the same dish while in the oven.

equipment

Juicer
Vegetable peeler

ingredients

Olive oil spray
4–6 medium potatoes, peeled
  and sliced thinly
Juice of 2 lemons

method

1. Preheat oven to 180°C (350°F/Gas mark 4). Spray a roasting dish lightly with olive oil spray and put in the potatoes in one layer. Spray potatoes with olive oil spray. Sprinkle with salt and pepper and sit the chicken on top, if using. Cook for about 1 hour.
2. Remove the chicken, if using, and pour the juice of two lemons over the potatoes. Turn oven heat up to 200°C (400°F/Gas mark 5) and cook until potatoes are golden and crispy on the edges.

Batter for Fish Fingers

This batter is perfect for flash-fried fish fingers (see following page) and banana fritters.

equipment

Sifter
Large mixing bowl
Wooden spoon

ingredients

½ cup plain flour
1/4 cup cornflour
1 teaspoon baking powder
¼ teaspoon salt
1 egg. beaten
½ cup (125ml) milk
¼ cup very cold soda water

method

1. Sift the flour, cornflour, baking powder and salt into a bowl. Make a well in the centre, add the beaten egg and milk. Stir well to combine.
2. Leave batter to stand for 20–30 minutes.
3. Stir in the cold soda water just before dipping the fish or fruit. Mix well to combine.

'They tell me there's fish in the ocean,
They tell me there's fish in the sea,
But I buy my fish in the fish shop
So it all sounds fishy to me.'
~ Unreal Banana Peel (p13)

Flash-Fried Fish Fingers with Baked Potato Chips

Preparation time: 15 minutes
Cooking time: 10 minutes for the fish, 30 minutes for the chips
Serves: 2

equipment

Kitchen knife
Measuring cups
Small bowl
Chopping board
Medium-large frying pan
Paper towels

ingredients

4 large potatoes, peeled
¼ cup olive oil
1–2 teaspoons salt
250g (8oz) flathead fillets
1 quantity batter
⅓ cup vegetable oil

method

1. Preheat oven to 230°C (210°C fan-forced/450°F/Gas mark 7).
2. Cut the potatoes into wedges about 1x1cm (¼x¼inch). Blanch in a large pan of boiling water for 3 minutes, drain and dry with paper towels.
3. Spread out evenly on a baking tray. Drizzle with olive oil and sprinkle over 1–2 teaspoons salt, coating each chip is evenly.
5. Bake for 20–30 minutes or until golden and crisp, turning potatoes a couple of times with tongs.
6. Meanwhile, cut the fish into strips, about 12cm (4½inches) long.
7. Dip the fish in the batter and shake off excess.
8. Just before cooking, heat the oil in the frying pan. Shallow fry the fillets around 3–5 minutes on each side, until golden and crisp. Serve with potato chips.

Mini Lamb Roast

My children always love a lamb roast. If you start with a mini roast, it's a good way to learn how to get the timing right.

Preparation time: 10 minutes
Cooking time: 20 minutes
Serves: 2

equipment

Kitchen paper towels
Chopping board
Kitchen knife
Small sharp knife
Food processor or blender
Small mixing bowl
Roasting tray
Aluminium foil

ingredients

1 mini lamb roast, 375g–400g (11½–13oz)
1 small clove garlic, peeled and sliced into slivers
Salt and freshly ground black pepper

herb crust

½ cup freshly chopped mixed herbs (such as mint, parsley, sage)
1 tablespoon Dijon mustard
1 tablespoon soy sauce

method

1. Preheat oven to 200°C (180°C fan-forced/400°F/gas mark 6).
2. Wipe meat dry with paper towels, insert slivers of garlic at various points with a small sharp knife. Season the lamb all over with salt and pepper.
3. Process the herbs, mustard and soy sauce in a blender or small food processor until herbs are finely chopped. Spread the paste over top and sides of lamb.
4. Roast in pre-heated oven for 18–20 minutes. Remove and cover with foil. Leave to rest ten minutes before carving. Drizzle meat with pan juices when serving.
5. For the vegetables: peel and chop two medium potatoes, 1 small kumara and 1 red onion into bite-size pieces. Place in a bowl and drizzle with olive oil, salt, pepper and chopped rosemary. Toss to combine well. Place on baking tray around the lamb and turn occasionally with tongs.

Mini Bat Wings

These mini chicken drumsticks are made from the fleshy part of the wing. (You might have noticed they're very popular in Harry Potter's "Potterverse"). You can use drumsticks if you prefer. Good to munch on or to take on a picnic.

Preparation time: 10 minutes
Standing time: 30 minutes
Cooking time: 20–25 minutes
Serves: 4 to 6

equipment

Measuring cups and spoons
Medium bowl
Plastic wrap
Garlic crusher
Grater
Baking paper
Baking tray

ingredients

1kg (2lb) mini chicken
  drumsticks or chicken wings
Cooking oil spray
Choose one of these three marinades:

Bali bliss

3 tablespoons kecap manis
  (sweet soy sauce)
3 tablespoons sweet chilli sauce
2 tablespoons vegetable oil
2 cloves garlic, crushed

The bee's knees

3 tablespoons soy sauce
2 tablespoons vegetable oil
1 tablespoon honey
2 cloves garlic, crushed
2 teaspoons grated ginger

BBQ-cause I can

½ cup barbecue sauce
1 tablespoon Worcestershire
  sauce
2 cloves garlic, crushed

method

1. Put drumsticks in a bowl, combine all ingredients for the marinade and pour over the chicken. Combine well.
2. Cover with plastic wrap and refrigerate for 15–20 minutes.
3. Preheat oven to 200°C (400°F/Gas mark 6).
4. Drain the chicken drumsticks and place on a baking tray lined with baking paper and sprayed with cooking oil. Cook in oven for 20–25 minutes or until cooked through and golden.
5. Remove from oven and leave to cool a little before devouring. Don't forget the napkins!

Stir-Fry Chicken & Noodles with Vegies

This is an easy and delicious stir-fry: just make sure you have everything chopped and ready before you start and then it will only take you a few minutes.

Preparation time: 15–20 minutes
Cooking time: 8 minutes
Serves: 4

equipment

Measuring cups and spoons
Medium bowl
Wok or large frying pan
Kitchen knife
Chopping board

ingredients

400g (13oz) soft hokkien noodles
1 tablespoon sesame oil
400g (13oz) chicken breast strips
4 green onions, white part only, sliced thinly
½ red capsicum, sliced thinly (optional)
1 bunch broccolini (or about 180g/6oz of snow peas), cut in 5cm lengths and steamed
1 medium cob of corn (about 250g/8oz), kernels only
2 tablespoons oyster sauce
1 tablespoon soy sauce
2–3 tablespoon chicken stock or water

Tip: You can substitute 20–24 medium green prawns (cleaned, deveined, tails left on) for the chicken

method

1. Soak the noodles in boiling water for 1–2 minutes. Drain and set aside.
2. Heat the wok, add the oil and swirl it around. Add chicken and stir-fry for 2–3 minutes or until golden all over. Add the green onions, capsicum, broccolini and corn kernels and stir-fry for one minute.
3. Add the drained noodles and toss well to combine. Add oyster sauce, soy sauce and chicken stock or water and mix well. Turn off the heat and cover with a lid for one minute.
4. Divide between 4 bowls or spoon into noodle boxes.

Stir-fry Beef with Vegetables

Preparation time: 15–20 minutes
Marinating time: 30–60 minutes
Cooking time: 8 minutes
Serves: 2

equipment

Measuring cups and spoons
Medium bowl
Wok or large frying pan
Kitchen knife
Chopping board
Vegetable peeler
Garlic crusher
Grater

ingredients

250g (8oz) rump steak, fat trimmed and sliced across the grain
1 tablespoon soy sauce or teriyaki marinade
1 teaspoon cornflour
1 teaspoon caster sugar
2 tablespoons vegetable oil
1 onion, cut into eighths
2 teaspoons finely grated fresh ginger
2 cloves garlic, peeled and chopped finely
1 carrot, peeled and sliced thinly
½ red or green capsicum, sliced
1 baby bok choy, washed and chopped
and/or 2 zucchini, sliced, or large handful snow peas, strings removed
1–2 tablespoon soy sauce, sweet chilli sauce or oyster sauce
¼ cup water or beef stock

Tip: It's important to have all your ingredients chopped and ready-to-go before you start stir-frying. Once the heat's on, that's it, you're up and running and there's no waiting around for dawdlers.

method

1. Put the steak into a bowl with the soy sauce, cornflour and sugar. Mix to combine and set aside for half an hour or one hour. This step gives the meat flavour and helps to tenderise it.
2. Heat a wok or large frying pan. Add 1 tablespoon of oil and stir fry the onions for 1 minute, then add the ginger and garlic. Stir-fry 30 seconds, then add the carrot and capsicum. Keep tossing and stirring.
3. Remove the vegetables to a plate and keep warm.
4. Heat remaining tablespoon oil in the wok. Stir-fry the meat in 2–3 batches until browned on all sides. Transfer each batch to a plate.
5. Return all the vegetables and meat to the pan. Add the bok choy, zucchini or snow peas, stir and toss to combine.
6. Add sauce and the stock or water. Put on the lid, turn down heat and leave to simmer for 1–2 minutes or until greens are just cooked. Serve with steamed rice.

Chicken Schnitzels

You can use lean veal (or pork) instead of the chicken, if you prefer, but I know that kids love the chicken version. Schnitzels are also good in a roll with salad and mayonnaise.

Preparation time: 15 minutes
Cooking time: 10 minutes
Serves: 4

equipment

Plastic wrap
Large heavy frying pan
Small bowl
2 plates
Baking tray

ingredients

4 x 125g (4oz) chicken
  schnitzels
Salt and pepper
½ cup plain flour
2 eggs, beaten with 2
  tablespoons cold water
1 cup dried breadcrumbs or
  panko breadcrumbs
30g (1oz) butter
2 tablespoons olive oil

Tip: For Parmesan Chicken Schnitzel, use ⅔ cup breadcrumbs and ⅓ cup grated parmesan cheese and ½ teaspoon paprika instead of plain breadcrumbs to coat. Baby lamb cutlets, trimmed of fat, are also delicious cooked like this and make excellent finger food.

main courses

method

1. Pat schnitzels dry with paper towels and season with salt and pepper. Dust schnitzels lightly with the flour. Dip each one into the beaten eggs allow excess egg to drip off. Dip into the breadcrumbs, firming them on with your hand.
2. Place on a tray in refrigerator, covered with plastic wrap for 15 minutes so that the coating stays on when cooked.
3. Heat oil and butter together in a frying pan over medium heat. Add 2 chicken schnitzels and cook 4–5 minutes on each side or until golden all over and cooked through. Remove to a warm place and cover. Reheat the oil and repeat with remaining chicken pieces.
4. Serve immediately with a wedge of lemon, steamed baby potatoes and a green salad.

Paula's Mini Meatloaves

These little meatloaves are perfect for the school lunchbox. Or slice them for meatloaf sandwiches.

Preparation time: 20–25 minutes
Cooking time: 30 minutes
Makes 8 x mini loaf tins or ovenproof dishes

equipment

Medium mixing bowl
Food processor or blender
Kitchen knife
Chopping board
Medium mixing bowl
Measuring cups and spoons
Egg slicer
Oven mitts
8 x mini loaf tins (3/4 cup size)
Pastry brush

ingredients

Cooking oil spray
500g (1lb) beef mince
250g (8oz) sausage mince
2 slices wholemeal or wholegrain bread, crusts trimmed
1 onion, peeled and finely chopped
1 carrot, peeled and finely chopped
1 zucchini, washed and finely chopped
1 tablespoon BBQ sauce
1 egg, beaten
1 teaspoon mixed dried herbs
1 teaspoon beef stock powder
Salt and freshly ground black pepper
4 boiled eggs (optional), sliced with an egg slicer

glaze
½ cup fruit chutney or BBQ sauce

method

1. Preheat oven to 190°C (170°C fan-forced/375°F/Gas mark 5). Spray mini loaf tins with cooking oil.
2. Place beef and sausage mince in a medium bowl.
3. Cut bread into quarters and place in food processor or blender. Process to make breadcrumbs.
4. Combine all the ingredients, except for the boiled eggs, and mix with your hands until well combined.
5. Spoon mixture into tins. If you are using the boiled eggs, spoon mixture into tins ¾ of the way to the top. Add a layer of sliced eggs, then top with more meat mixture.
6. Cook in oven for 20 minutes. Using oven mitts, remove tins from oven and strain off juices—ask an adult for help with this.
7. Brush tops with fruit chutney or BBQ sauce. Return to oven for another 10 minutes. Delicious served hot or cold.

desserts

'The Magic Pudding is a pie, except when it is something else, like a steak, or a jam donut, or an apple dumpling, or whatever its owner wants it to be. And it never runs out. No matter how many slices you cut, there's always something left over. It's magic.'

- The Magic Pudding by Norman Lindsay

Fresh Fruit with White Chocolate Dip

This is one of the most luxurious ways to eat fruit—though I wouldn't recommend you do it every day!

Preparation: 15–20 minutes
Cooking: 5–10 minutes
Serves: 4

equipment

Serving platter
Medium saucepan
Small serving bowl
Chopping board
Kitchen knife
Whisk
Wooden cocktail skewers

ingredients

1 large banana, peeled and
  sliced into 4 pieces
16 whole strawberries
250g (8oz) seedless grapes,
  stems removed
    or 2 kiwi fruit, peeled and cut
  into cubes

the dip

½ cup (125ml/4fl oz) pouring
  cream
1 teaspoon finely grated orange
  zest
200g (6oz) white chocolate,
  chopped
2 tablespoons freshly squeezed
  orange juice, strained
Extra cream, as required

Tips: Substitute a good quality dark chocolate for the white chocolate. If making this for mum or dad, you can use an orange liqueur such as Grand Marnier or Cointreau instead of the orange juice. Be sure to ask their permission first!

method

1. Arrange the fruit on a serving platter.
2. Place the cream in a medium saucepan and bring to simmering point. Add the orange zest and chocolate. Whisk over low heat until smooth and then add the orange juice. Be careful not to overheat as it will cause the chocolate to separate. If the mixture is too thick, add more cream.
3. Spoon dip into a small serving bowl, suitable for dipping, and serve alongside fruit.

Rainbow Fruit Cake

This is a wonderfully simple dessert which you can make with a variety of fruits. A great one to make for Mum for Mother's Day.

Preparation time: 40 minutes
Standing time: 4 hours
Serves: 8–10

equipment

Large flat serving platter or tray
  (about 26x40cm/9x16inches)
Measuring cups and spoons
Small knife
Juice squeezer
Medium bowls
Small saucepan
Teaspoon
Spatula
Medium pastry brush
Wooden spoon
Medium sieve

ingredients

¾ cup (185ml/6fl oz) freshly
  squeezed orange juice
2 tablespoons brown sugar
250g (8oz) savoiardi biscuits
  (Italian sponge fingers)
500ml good quality vanilla
  yoghurt (or use your favourite
  flavour yoghurt)

the topping

3 medium peaches, peeled,
  stoned and cut into eighths,
  (or 400g/12oz can peaches,
  drained)
1 punnet strawberries, hulled
  and sliced
1 punnet blueberries
3 kiwi fruit, peeled and sliced
2 medium bananas, sliced into
  ½cm(¼inch) rounds
2 passionfruit, halved

the glaze

½ cup smooth apricot jam
Juice of ½ lemon

*Somewhere over the rainbow
way up high,
There's a land that I heard of
Once in a lullaby.*

~E.Y. Harburg

desserts

method

1. To make the base, mix together the orange juice and brown sugar in a bowl. Stir until sugar is dissolved. Dip the biscuits one by one in the liquid (watch they don't go too soggy) and lay them flat on the platter in neat rows.

2. Spread the yoghurt evenly over the biscuits.
3. Start making the rainbow with a row of sliced strawberries in one of the corners.
4. Follow this with a curved line of blueberries then kiwifruit, bananas and peaches. Keep alternating lines of fruit until you have covered the top.

5. Using a teaspoon, spoon the passionfruit evenly over the banana slices.
6. For the glaze: combine the apricot jam and lemon juice in a small saucepan and bring to the boil over low heat, stirring with a wooden spoon. Strain through a sieve into a bowl. Brush the glaze lightly over the fruit.

7. Cover with plastic wrap and refrigerate for 3–4 hours. Remove from refrigerator about 30 minutes before serving.

Echidna Pavlova

This cute pavlova is shaped like an echidna!

Preparation time: 25 minutes
Cooking time: 1½ hours
Serves: 6–8

equipment

Measuring cups and spoons
Baking tray
Baking paper
Mixmaster or electric beaters
Spatula
Chopping board
Kitchen knife
Juice squeezer

ingredients

4 egg whites
200g (1 cup) caster sugar
1 teaspoon white vinegar
1 teaspoon vanilla essence
1 tablespoon cornflour
400ml (14fl oz) thickened
  cream, stiffly whipped
1kg (2lb) fresh summer stone
  fruit: apricots, nectarines,
  peaches, plums (or fruits
  in season)
3 tablespoons toasted slivered
  almonds
Freshly squeezed lemon juice
1 red seedless grape (for
  the eyes)

method

1. Preheat oven to low (120°C/100°C fan-forced/250°F/ Gas mark 1). Line a baking tray with non-stick paper.
2. In a mixing bowl, whisk egg whites with half the sugar until stiff and shiny. Fold in remaining sugar, vinegar, vanilla and cornflour. Spoon mixture onto prepared tray to make an oval shape, giving it a slightly elongated shape at one end (this is the echidna's face).
3. Bake for one hour, turn off oven, leaving pavlova in for another half hour. Remove and leave to cool completely.
4. Wash the fruit and cut into halves. Remove seeds. Cut flesh into matchsticks (batons) about 5mm thick. Toss batons in a little lemon juice to stop them from turning brown. Cover pavlova with the stiffly whipped cream. Place fruit sticks and slivered almonds upright into the cream to resemble echidna spines.
5. Cut a red seedless grape in half for the eyes.

Lemon Delicious ..is very very delicious

This must be one of the very best desserts and is a family favourite!

Preparation time: 15 minutes
Cooking time: 50 minutes
Serves: 4

equipment

1½L (48fl oz) ovenproof
  pudding dish
or 4 small individual ovenproof
  dishes
Measuring cups and spoons
Mixmaster or electric beaters
Grater or microplane
Spatula
Deep baking tray

ingredients

60g (2oz) softened butter
Zest and juice of 2 medium
  lemons
1 cup (220g/7oz) caster sugar
3 tablespoons self-raising flour,
  sifted
3 free range or organic eggs,
  separated
1½ cups (375ml/12fl oz) milk

method

1. Preheat oven to 180°C (160°C fan-forced/350°F/Gas mark 4).
   Grease pudding dish or individual ovenproof dishes.
2. Cream together the butter, lemon zest and sugar. Add the egg
   yolks.
3. Beat in flour and milk alternately to make a smooth batter.
   Scrape down around the sides and pour in the lemon juice.
   Blend to combine.
4. In another bowl, whisk the egg whites with electric beaters until
   they form soft peaks. Fold gently through the lemon batter.
* Ask an adult to help with the next step
5. Pour mixture into prepared dish or dishes. Place in a deep
   baking tray and pour in enough hot water to come about
   one-third of the way up the sides of the dish. Bake for 50–60
   minutes or until golden and just set. Cover with foil if it is
   browning too quickly.
6. Leave to cool a little before serving. Dust with icing sugar.
   Delicious served with fresh cream.

Apple Crumble

There's nothing better than a juicy apple just picked from the tree. When apples are in season, make the best of them with this popular dessert. Young children love to help with the crumble

Preparation time: 20 minutes
Cooking time: 30–40 minutes
Serves: 4–6

equipment

Chopping board
Kitchen knife
Vegetable peeler
Fruit juicer
Measuring cups and spoons
Spatula
1½L (48fl oz) litre ovenproof
　pudding dish
Medium saucepan

ingredients

1kg (2lb) Granny Smith apples,
　peeled and sliced
2 tablespoons water or fresh
　orange juice
2 tablespoons caster sugar
3–4 cloves

crumble

100g (3oz) cold butter, diced
¾ cup self-raising flour
1 teaspoon cinnamon
¾ cup brown sugar
⅓ cup (30g) desiccated coconut
⅓ cup (30g) rolled oats

method

1. Put the apples in a pan with water or juice, sugar and cloves. Cover and cook over medium-low heat until apples are soft. Spoon apples and cooking juices into an ovenproof serving dish.
2. Preheat oven to 180°C (160°C fan-forced/350°F/Gas mark 4).
3. In a medium bowl, rub butter into flour with your fingertips until mixture resembles fine breadcrumbs. Add cinnamon, sugar, coconut and rolled oats and mix through. Or place all crumble ingredients in a food processor or blender and process until combined.
4. Spread crumble over the apple filling. Bake for 30–40 minutes or until golden. Serve with vanilla ice cream.

> Tip: When stone fruits are in season, use a mixture of these (peaches, apricots, plums, nectarines) instead of the apples: wash well, cut in half and remove the stones, then slice into pieces. Substitute a cinnamon stick for the cloves.

Here is the tree with leaves so green,
Here are the apples that hang between;
When the wind blows, the apples fall,
Here is a basket to gather them all.

Easy Peasy Butter Cake

This simple basic mixture is very versatile because it can be used to make cupcakes, patty cakes or a slab cake.

Preparation time: 15 minutes
Cooking time: 20–25 minutes
Serves: 12

equipment

Measuring cups and spoons
Sifter
Mixmaster or electric beaters
Mixing bowl
Spatula
22cm (8½inch) round cake tin

ingredients

125g (4oz) very soft butter
¾ cup (185g/6oz) sugar
2 eggs, at room temperature
1⅔ cup (250g/8oz) self raising
  flour, sifted
½ cup (125ml/4fl oz) milk
Pinch salt
1 teaspoon vanilla essence

method

1. Preheat oven to 180°C (160°C fan-forced/350°F/Gas mark 4). Grease the cake tin (I used one with a 'happy birthday' imprint).
2. Put all the ingredients into a mixing bowl and, using electric beaters, beat on high speed for three minutes.
3. Spoon mixture into tin and bake 40–45 minutes or until risen and a light gold colour. Remove from oven and set aside to cool. Leave in tin for 10 minutes before turning out.
4. Spread with chocolate ganache (page 162). Dust with icing sugar and decorate.

This mixture will also make 12 cupcakes—line ⅓ cup muffin tins with paper cases and spoon in mixture. Bake in moderate oven for 20–25 minutes. For chocolate cupcakes, add 2 tablespoons cocoa sifted with the flour and stir through ½ cup choc chips at the end.

Marble Birthday Cake

This makes a big cake, perfect for a birthday party. Serve with Neapolitan ice cream for a perfect colour match.

Preparation time: 30 minutes
Cooking time: 1 hour
Serves: 10–12

equipment

Measuring cups and spoons
Sifter
Mixmaster or electric beaters
Mixing bowl
Spatula
Deep 25cm (10 inch) diameter
  cake tin
Baking paper

ingredients

250g (8oz) very soft butter
1½ cups (370g/12oz) sugar
4 eggs, lightly beaten
3¼ cups (480g/15oz) self
  raising flour, sifted
1 cup (250ml/8fl oz) milk
Pinch salt
2 teaspoons vanilla
Pink food colouring
2 tablespoons cocoa
1- 2 tablespoons milk

method

1. Preheat oven to 180°C (160°C fan-forced/350°F/Gas mark 4). Line the bottom and sides of cake tin with baking paper.
2. Combine butter, sugar, eggs, flour, milk, salt and vanilla in a mixing bowl. Using electric beaters, beat on high speed for three minutes.
3. Divide batter evenly between three bowls:
   Bowl one: leave this mixture untouched
   Bowl two: add a few drops of pink food colouring to this bowl and stir to combine.
   Bowl three: blend 2 tablespoons cocoa with 1–2 tablespoons milk and stir through the third bowl of batter.
4. Drop alternate spoonfuls of the three colours into the tin. Swirl a skewer through the mixture a few times to give a marbled effect. Gently tap tin on bench and smooth the surface.
5. Bake, uncovered, for 1 hour 10 minutes. Test with a skewer; if the skewer comes out clean, the cake is done.
6. Ice with Rocky Road Icing (page 144) or your favourite icing.

Rocky Road Icing

equipment

Heatproof bowl
Saucepan
Spatula

ingredients

400g (13oz) milk or dark
  chocolate
200g (6oz) mini pink and white
  marshmallows
½ cup shredded coconut
Handful of chopped walnuts or
  macadamias (optional)

method

1. Melt chocolate in a heatproof bowl set over a saucepan
   of boiling water. Stir gently with a spatula, being careful
   not to overheat.
2. Remove bowl from heat and stir in marshmallows and coconut.
3. Spread immediately over your cake and sprinkle with chopped
   walnuts or macadamias. Set aside until chocolate has
   hardened—it will be easier to cut if refrigerated for 10–15
   minutes.

Chocolate Buttermilk Cake with Chocolate Ganache

This is a lovely moist cake and the cinnamon gives it a wonderful aroma.

Preparation time: 15–20 minutes
Cooking time: 45–50 minutes

equipment

Chopping board
Kitchen knife
Measuring cups and spoons
Mixmaster or electric beater
Mixing bowl
Steel bowl
Saucepan
Spatula
3L (96fl oz) bundt tin (tin with a
  hole in the centre)

ingredients

250g (8oz) softened butter,
  roughly chopped
1½ cups (335g/10½oz) sugar
3 free range or organic eggs
1 teaspoon vanilla
3 cups (450g) plain flour
½ cup cocoa
2 teaspoons bi-carbonate soda
1½ teaspoons cinnamon
  (optional)
2 cups (500ml/16fl oz)
  buttermilk

chocolate ganache

½ cup (125ml/4fl oz) pouring
  cream
300g (10oz) dark or milk
  chocolate, broken into pieces

146 *desserts*

method

1. Preheat oven to 180°C(160°C fan-forced/350°F/Gas mark 4). Grease and flour a bundt tin.
2. In a medium bowl, cream the butter and sugar using electric beaters, add the eggs one at a time, then add the vanilla. In a separate bowl, sift together the flour, cocoa, bi-carbonate soda and cinnamon. Add sifted mixture to butter mixture, alternating with the buttermilk and beat well after each addition.
3. Pour mixture into prepared tin and cook in oven 45–50 minutes or until a skewer inserted into the cake comes out clean. Leave in cake tin for 10 minutes before turning out onto a cake rack.

ganache

1. Place chocolate pieces in a heatproof bowl.
2. In a small saucepan, bring cream to boiling point.
3. Remove cream from heat and pour over the chocolate. Stir vigorously with a wooden spoon until smooth and glossy. Leave to cool for a few minutes.
4. Pour over cake on cake rack, smoothing sides with a spatula. Top cake with shredded coconut (optional).

Watermelon Fruit Salad Basket

This makes a very pretty presentation for a birthday party, barbecue or any outdoor meal. Choose your watermelon carefully. It should be a lovely round shape. Then select your favourite fruit—the ones listed are suggestions only. Please ask an adult to cut the basket shape for you as this requires a large knife.

Preparation time: 45 minutes

equipment

Felt-tip pen
Kitchen knife
Small sharp knife
Chopping board
4–5 medium bowls
Damp kitchen wipe
Melon baller
Fruit juicer

ingredients

1 round seedless watermelon, about 5–6kg (10–12lb)
½ rockmelon/cantaloupe, seeds removed
½ honeydew melon, seeds removed
1–2 bananas, peeled and sliced
2 kiwi fruit, peeled and sliced
2 mangoes, cheeks removed and flesh sliced
1 punnet strawberries, hulled, and sliced
4–6 passionfruit (pulp only)
Juice of one lemon
Mint leaves, for garnishing

Tips: To prevent the fruit salad becoming soggy, make a few small drainage holes in the bottom after you have hollowed it out and before filling with fruit.
A small wad of damp paper towel placed underneath will keep it stable.

method

1. Slice a small thin piece off the bottom of the melon so that it sits flat. Wipe the skin clean with a damp cloth, then sit the base on the cloth.

2. Use a felt-tip pen to mark out the shape of the basket but leave a strip of about 5cm wide that will form the handle of your basket. Ask an adult to cut out the shape using a large kitchen knife.

3. Using a melon baller, scoop balls of the flesh from the melons, placing the different colours in different bowls. The melons will be quite watery and need to be drained regularly over the sink. Hollow out the inside of the watermelon with a spoon, gently scraping the sides of the basket. Be careful when removing flesh from the handle as you don't want it to break.

4. Once all the flesh is scooped out, use a small knife to make small 'V' shapes all around the sides of the basket and along the handle (this step is optional).

5. Combine equal quantities of melon balls in one medium large bowl. Add remaining fruits and lemon juice and toss well to combine. Spoon fruit salad into the basket and decorate with mint leaves.

desserts

edible
gifts

'"Then you should say what you mean," the March Hare went on. "I do," Alice hastily replied; "at least I mean what I say, that's the same thing, you know."
"Not the same thing a bit!" said the Hatter. "Why, you might just as well say that I see what I eat is the same thing as I eat what I see!".'

~ *Alice in Wonderland* by Lewis Carroll

Red Velvet Cupcakes

These cupcakes are named because they are served on the red carpet to the stars and also because of their texture and moistness. This is due to the reaction of the buttermilk with vinegar and bi-carb soda. If you like the red colour, add another teaspoon of cochineal.

Preparation time: 15 minutes
Cooking time: 20 minutes
Makes 24

equipment

Measuring cups and spoons
Electric beaters
Sifter
Spatula
Skewer
2 x 12-hole muffin tins
24 paper cases

ingredients

1½ cups (335g/10½oz) caster sugar
1½ cups (375ml/12fl oz) vegetable oil
2 free range eggs, at room temperature
1 teaspoon vanilla
1 teaspoon cochineal (red food colouring)
2½ cups (375g/12oz) plain flour
3 tablespoons cocoa
1 teaspoon salt
¾ teaspoon baking powder
1 cup (250ml/8fl oz) buttermilk
2 teaspoons white vinegar
¾ teaspoon bi-carbonate of soda

frosting

60g (2oz) softened butter
185g (6¼oz) softened cream cheese
1–2 teaspoons vanilla essence
1½ cups (250g/8oz) sifted icing sugar

method

1. Preheat oven to 180°C (160°C fan-forced/350°F/Gas mark 4). Line muffin tins with paper cases.
2. Using electric beaters, beat together the sugar and oil on high speed until combined. Add eggs one at a time. Add vanilla and food colouring. Scrape down sides of mixing bowl with the spatula when necessary.
3. In a separate bowl, sift together the flour, cocoa, salt and baking powder. Add this to the sugar mixture in three batches, alternating with the buttermilk. Beat well to combine after each addition.
4. In a small bowl, stir together the vinegar and bi-carbonate of soda until it foams. Add to the sugar and flour mixture and beat well to combine.
5. Spoon the batter into prepared muffin cups, filling each three-quarters full. Bake for 20 minutes or until a skewer inserted in the centre comes out clean.
6. Meanwhile, make the frosting by beating the butter and cream cheese together until well combined. Add vanilla essence. Sift in the icing sugar—use enough to achieve the consistency you like. Spread cupcakes with frosting when they are done. This makes 1½ cups.

Tip: To make cupcake cones, remove paper cups from cupcakes and trim bottoms to fit into flat-bottomed cones. Place a few lollies in each cupcake cone, then insert the cupcake, pushing it down gently to secure it. Using a small spatula, spread tops with frosting and stud with Smarties.

Red Velvet Cupcakes

Cupcake Cones

Marshmallows

Just make sure you give these a good beating, and they should turn out well.

Preparation time: 15–20 minutes
Cooking time: 20 minutes
Makes about 40 small marshmallows

equipment

Measuring cups and bowls
Small bowl
Medium-large saucepan
Electric mixer and mixing bowl
Slab or lamington tin

ingredients

2 tablespoons powdered
  gelatine
½ cup (125ml/4fl oz) cold water
2 cups (440g/14oz) sugar
1 cup (250ml/8fl oz) boiling
  water
1 teaspoon vanilla essence
1 cup desiccated coconut

method

1. Sprinkle gelatine over cold water in a small bowl, making sure it all gets wet. If gelatine hardens, place in microwave for 20 seconds or until it becomes liquid again.
2. Put the sugar and boiling water into a large heavy saucepan and stir over moderate heat until sugar is dissolved. Add the gelatine mixture and boil for 20 minutes, uncovered. Remove from the heat and cool to lukewarm.
3. Pour the mixture into a large mixing bowl, add the vanilla essence and beat rapidly until very thick and white. It's a good idea to cover the mixmaster with a damp tea towel to prevent the bench-top from being sprayed with the mixture.
4. Pour into a slab or lamington tin which has been rinsed out with cold water. Refrigerate until set.
5. Cut into squares with a knife dipped in warm water, then toss each piece in coconut.

Tip: You can colour half the mixture pink and the other half green if you like. Or roll in coloured coconut by putting desiccated coconut in a plastic bag and rubbing through a few drops of the food colouring.

Marshmallows

Afghan Biscuits

Afghan Biscuits (or Yum Yums)

These buttery, crunchy chocolate biscuits are very popular in New Zealand. The origin of the name is unknown, but I can guarantee they are very yum.

Preparation time: 15 minutes
Cooking time: 15–20 minutes
Makes about 20

equipment

Mixmaster or electric beater
Measuring cups and spoons
Spatula
Baking trays
Baking paper
Cake rack

ingredients

200g (6½oz) softened unsalted butter
½ cup (110g/4oz) sugar
1¼ cups (185g/6oz) plain flour
¼ cup (25g/1oz) cocoa
2 cups (100g/3½oz) cornflakes
Whole walnuts or pecans

chocolate glaze

75g (2½oz) dark chocolate, broken up
60g (2oz) unsalted butter
1 teaspoon honey

method

1. Preheat oven to 180°C (160°C fan-forced/350°F/Gas mark 4). Line a baking tray with baking paper.
2. In a large mixing bowl, cream together the butter and sugar until light and fluffy. In a separate bowl, sift together the flour and cocoa and fold into the butter mixture. Lightly crush the cornflakes in your hands then stir them through the chocolate mixture—it will be a bit stiff so do it carefully.
3. Use your hands to shape the mixture into balls about the size of a large walnut, put each ball on a tray about 3cm apart, then gently press them flat.
4. Bake in oven for 15–20 minutes. Leave on tray for 10 minutes then transfer to a wire rack to cool.
5. While the biscuits are cooling, make the glaze: place the chocolate, butter and honey into a small heatproof bowl set over a saucepan of simmering water. Stir until smooth and glossy. Remove bowl from heat.
6. When biscuits are cool, spoon a little of the chocolate glaze over each one and top with a pecan or walnut.

Gingerbread Men

You can make whatever shape you like with this gingerbread dough: gingerbread men of all sizes, reindeer, cockatoos, bells, angels, stars.

Makes about 20 men, or enough for a Gingerbread House.

equipment

Mixmaster or electric beaters
Mixing bowl
Spatula
Sifter
Small saucepan
Plastic wrap
Baking trays lined with baking
  paper
Cookie cutter

ingredients

250g (8oz) softened butter
185g (6oz) brown sugar
2 organic or free range eggs
300ml (10fl oz) honey
750g–800g (1½–1¾lb) plain flour
Pinch salt
3 teaspoons ground ginger
2 teaspoons cinnamon
½ teaspoon allspice
3 teaspoons bi-carbonate
  of soda dissolved in 125ml
  (4fl oz) boiling water
Royal icing (see page 172)

method

1. Cream together the butter and sugar until light. Beat in the eggs one at a time then add the honey.
2. Sift together the dry ingredients and add to the creamed mixture alternately with dissolved bi-carbonate soda. If the dough feels too soft, add a little more flour. Shape into a ball and wrap in greaseproof paper or plastic wrap. Refrigerate two hours or overnight.
3. Preheat oven to 180°C (160°C fan-forced/350°F/gas mark 4).
4. Divide the gingerbread into four so that you can work with one piece at a time, putting the remainder back (wrapped) into the refrigerator. Roll out onto a lightly floured board and stamp out shapes with a cutter. Lift carefully onto greased baking trays.
5. Bake for about 15 minutes or until browned. Remove with a spatula to cool on a wire rack. Decorate with smarties for eyes, jellybeans (mouth) and coconut (hair). Or spoon royal icing into a piping bag with a small nozzle and pipe squiggles over the men or other shapes .

Tip: It's easier to measure honey if you warm it first in the microwave. Be careful not to overheat it or to burn yourself.

Gingerbread Men

Rose Friands

Rose Friends

These lovely moist little cakes are perfect to make for Mum for morning or afternoon tea on Mother's Day. If you don't have rose-shaped tins, bake them in muffin tins.

Preparation time: 15 minutes
Cooking time: 30 minutes
Makes 12

equipment

Small saucepan
Mixing bowl
Sifter
12 rose-shaped tins or ⅓ cup muffin tins
Wooden spoon

ingredients

Cooking oil spray
160g unsalted butter
1 cup (110g/3½oz) ground almonds
1½ cups (200g/6½oz) icing sugar
65g (⅓ cup plus 1 tbsp) plain flour
5 egg whites

Rose Cake Syrup
¼ cup freshly squeezed lemon or lime juice
4 tablespoons caster sugar
1 teaspoon rosewater

method

1. Preheat oven to 200°C (180°C fan-forced/400°F/gas mark 6). Spray 12 friand tins (or ½ cup muffin tins) with cooking oil spray.
2. Melt the butter in a saucepan and simmer gently until it deepens in colour. Remove from heat and leave to cool for five minutes.
3. Meanwhile sift the icing sugar and flour into a large bowl. Add the ground almonds and mix well. Stir in the egg whites (don't beat them) and mix to make a soft batter.
4. Pour the melted butter through a fine sieve into the batter and mix thoroughly. Spoon the mixture into the tins to about ¾ full.
5. Place in pre-heated oven and bake for five minutes.
6. Lower the temperature to 180°C (160°C fan-forced/350°F/gas mark 4) and bake for a further 20–25 minutes, covering the cakes if they are browning
7. Turn the oven off and leave the friands inside for five minutes. Cool for 10–15 minutes in the tin and then turn onto a rack.
8. Brush the cakes with Rose Syrup. Dust with icing sugar before serving.

Rose Cake Syrup:

1. Combine the lemon juice and sugar in a small pan over low heat. Bring to simmering point, stirring with a wooden spoon until sugar is dissolved.
2. Remove from heat and add the rosewater. Brush over the warm cakes.
3. Scatter with pesticide-free rose petals.

Face Cookies

Young children have a lot of fun decorating these biscuits.

Preparation time: 30 minutes
Makes 16

equipment

Two medium bowls
Spatula

ingredients

16 oval sweet biscuits (such as
  Arrowroot biscuits)
Blue and red food dyes
Royal icing (page 172)
M&Ms, Smarties, cachous for
  decorating
Shredded coconut

method

1. Divide icing in two portions and spoon into separate bowls. Add a few drops of different food dye to each bowl and stir well to combine.
2. Spread icing evenly over biscuit tops using a small spatula (dipped occasionally in hot water).
3. Decorate with M&Ms, Smarties, cachous to make a pretty face. Use shredded coconut for hair.

Royal Icing

Use this for Gingerbread, Arrowroot biscuit faces and to spread over your cupcakes – use a spatula and do it before it begins to set like concrete! Decorate tops with candied flowers, hearts, 100s& 1000s or whatever takes your fancy.

Preparation time: 10 – 15 minutes

equipment

Mixing bowl and beaters
Sifter
Spatula

ingredients

2 eggwhites, lightly beaten
3 cups pure icing sugar, sifted
Squeeze of lemon juice

method

1. Using an electric mixer, beat the egg whites until soft peaks form.
2. Gradually add the icing sugar, beating constantly until thick. When you lift the beaters, the icing mixture should look like soft snow peaks. Beat in the lemon juice.

Natali's Triple Chocolate Brownies

Preparation time: 15 minutes
Cooking time: 20–25 minutes
Makes 18 brownies

equipment

Measuring cups and spoons
Medium heatproof bowl
Medium saucepan
Spatula
Sifter
Kitchen knife
Slice or slab tin
  (20x30cm/8x12inches)
Baking paper

ingredients

300g (10oz) dark or milk
  chocolate, chopped
125g (4oz) unsalted butter,
  chopped
¾ cup (180g/6oz) caster sugar
2 free-range eggs, beaten
1 cup (150g) plain flour, sifted
100g (3½oz) white Choc Bits
2 packets chocolate Rolos
  (chilled)

method

1. Preheat oven to 180°C (160°C fan-forced/350°F/Gas mark 4).
   Line base and sides of slab tin with baking paper.
2. Place chocolate, butter and sugar in a heatproof bowl set over a
   pan of simmering water. Stir until chocolate and butter have melted.
3. Remove from heat and leave to cool for 5–10 minutes. Stir in
   the eggs. Mix in the flour, then stir in the white chocolate bits.
4. Spoon into prepared tin. Use a small knife to mark out 18
   squares and place a Rolo in each, pushing it into the mixture.
   Bake for 20–25 minutes.
5. Allow to cool for 10–15 minutes before cutting into pieces.

Shortbread

These are easy one to make for Christmas gifts – buttery and delicious.

Preparation time: 12 minutes
Cooking time: 30 minutes
Makes 30

equipment

Lamington tin
Steel bowl
Saucepan
Electric beaters
Spatula

ingredients

250g (8oz) unsalted butter
⅓ cup (45g) icing sugar
⅓ cup (45g) cornflour
¼ cup (50g) caster sugar
2 ⅓ cups (330g) plain flour
½ teaspoon vanilla essence

method

1. Preheat oven to 180°C (160°C fan-forced/350°F/Gas mark 4). Grease or line a lamington tin with non-stick baking paper.
2. Melt the butter over low heat and allow to cool a little. Sift the icing sugar, cornflour, caster sugar and plain flour into a bowl. Pour in the melted butter, add the vanilla essence and mix well to combine.
3. Press the mixture into the lamington tin and smooth the top with the palm of your hand. Mark into 30 fingers with a knife and prick all over with a fork. Press fork prongs into sides to make indentations.
4. Bake for 30 minutes or until a pale gold colour. Cut into 'fingers' while warm.
5. Store in airtight containers when cold. Wrap in cellophane or pretty Christmas paper and tie with a bow.

drinks and ices

'If all the world were apple pie
And all the sea were ink
And all the trees were bread and cheese?
What would we have to drink?'

~ *Nursery Rhyme*

Homemade Lemonade

Preparation time: 10 minutes
Cooking time: 5 minutes

equipment

Measuring cups and spoons
Medium saucepan
Zester or microplane
Chopping board
Kitchen knife
Fruit juicer
Strainer

ingredients

1 cup (200g/7oz) caster sugar
½ cup (125ml/4fl oz) water
Finely grated zest of 1 lemon
Juice of 3 lemons

method

1. Combine sugar, water and zest in a pan and simmer for five minutes or until the sugar is dissolved and you have a light syrup.
2. Strain the lemon juice and stir into the syrup. Cool and keep in the fridge.
3. Pour about a centimetre of the syrup into a glass and add ice and fizzy or still water, to taste.

Mixed Berry Smoothie

Smoothies (a blend of fruit, milk, ice cream or ice) are the ultimate fast food. You don't have to stick with full-cream milk - try a light variety or use buttermilk or yoghurt or one of the cultured milk drinks for a delicious tang.

Preparation time: 5 minutes
Makes 1 large smoothie

equipment

Blender or food processor
Measuring cups and spoons

ingredients

1 cup (250ml/8fl oz) milk
2 scoops ice cream
½ cup frozen berries
   (strawberries, raspberries,
   blueberries).
1–2 teaspoons honey, or sugar,
   to taste

method

1. Combine all ingredients in a blender and whiz until smooth and thick. Pour into a long soda glass and drink immediately.

Fruit Frappés

Use seasonal fruits for making fresh fruit frappés. Try different combinations such as mango, passionfruit and strawberry; peach and raspberry; or honeydew melon and ginger. The following are guidelines—use your imagination to create other combinations.

Preparation time: 5 minutes

equipment

Medium mixing bowl
Chopping board
Kitchen knife
Fruit juicer
Strainer
Jug
Blender
Crushed ice or ice blocks

ingredients

sugar syrup

200g (6oz) caster sugar
250ml (8oz) boiling water
Juice of ½ lemon or lime,
  strained

Tip: If you make the sugar syrup ahead of time and store it in the refrigerator, it's easy to whiz one up any time. Some people omit the syrup altogether, but it does bring out the flavour in the fruit. Make sure you taste the frappé first though, as some fruits are sweeter than others.

method

for the sugar syrup

1. Put the sugar into a bowl. Pour over the boiling water and stir until dissolved. Leave to cool.

2. Stir through the lemon or lime juice. Pour into a jug, cover and store in the refrigerator.

for the frappés

Makes one drink

- Watermelon Frappé: Combine 1½ cups cubed seedless watermelon flesh and 1 cup crushed ice in a blender and blend until smooth. Add sugar syrup to taste. Watermelon is also delicious mixed with pineapple (and mint) or with strawberries and crushed ice.

- Pineapple and Mint Frappé: Combine 1–1½ cups cubed pineapple, 1 cup crushed ice, 1–2 tablespoons sugar syrup and 4–6 fresh, finely sliced mint leaves in a blender and whiz until thick and smooth. Add sugar syrup to taste.

- Rockmelon Frappé: Whiz 1½ cups cubed rockmelon, 1 cup crushed ice, 1 tablespoon sugar syrup in a blender until thick and smooth. The pulp of a passionfruit is also a good addition.

- Raspberry and Peach Frappé: Combine the flesh of 1 large peach (preferably white), ¼ punnet raspberries and a cup of crushed ice in a blender and blend until smooth. Add sugar syrup to taste.

- Strawberry and Mango Frappé. Combine the flesh of one mango, 8 large strawberries (hulled) and a cup of crushed ice in a blender and blend until smooth. Add sugar syrup to taste.

Tutti Frutti Ice Blocks

On hot afternoons after school, these colourful healthy ice blocks are just the thing to cool you down.

Preparation time: 20 minutes
Freezing time: overnight
Makes 6 x 250ml (8fl oz) ice blocks

equipment

Chopping board
Kitchen knife
Medium mixing bowl
Fruit juicer
Plastic or take-away cups
Paddle pop sticks

ingredients

650g (19oz) mixed summer
  fruits
500ml (16fl oz) freshly squeezed
  orange juice or sparkling
  apple juice

method

1. Choose from a mixture of summer fruits including pineapple, paw paw, banana, passionfruit, mango, watermelon, peaches and nectarines.

2. Peel those that require peeling (do this over a bowl to catch the juices) and cut into bite-size pieces, removing any seeds as you go. Put into the bowl with the juices and toss well together, adding passionfruit pulp to taste.

3. Spoon mixture into plastic cups until about two-thirds full. Top up with freshly squeezed orange juice. Insert a paddle pop stick into each one and freeze overnight.

4. Remove from freezer about 5–10 minutes before serving. Run the cups briefly under warm water to release them, then give the ices a good pull.

Sunflower Ice Bowl

This is a really stunning thing to make in summer, especially for pool parties.

Preparation: 10 minutes
Freezing time: overnight

equipment

1 large plastic bowl
1 medium plastic bowl

Note: You need two plastic bowls, one smaller than the other —the smaller one must fit neatly into the larger one. Be sure to use a clear plastic outer bowl so that you can see where the flowers are to be positioned.

ingredients

Sunflowers (or flowers and leaves of choice)
Water

method

1. Fill the smaller bowl to the three quarter mark with water.
2. Place it inside the large bowl. There should be a gap of about 3 centimetres between the bowls: fill this gap with flowers and leaves of your choice (sunflowers look spectacular), or try slices of lemon and orange interspersed with leaves.
3. Using a jug, fill the gap between the two bowls with water. Carefully place bowls in the freezer overnight.
4. Next day, remove from freezer and let sit for 15–20 minutes before unmoulding. You may need to quickly plunge the outer bowl in a basin of warm water. Ease away the small bowl, then remove the larger one. Sit it on a small wad of wet kitchen paper on a secure drip-proof stand and fill with tutti fruity ice-blocks (see previous recipe)

about the author

A graduate of Leith's School of Food & Wine, London, Sheridan Rogers has over 30 years' industry experience. She conducts cooking classes for adults and children from her home, and has worked on many TV and magazine commercials as a food stylist and presenter.

As a food writer and journalist, Sheridan has worked on several leading newspapers and as a broadcaster she has contributed to a number of leading Sydney radio programs.

Sheridan has won a number of awards for her food writing including the 'Award for Gastronomic Writing', 'Best Show Story Award for the Royal Easter Show Media Awards' and the 'Best Hardcover Book for the Food Media Club Awards'.

index of recipes

First published in Australia in 2010 by New Holland Publishers (Australia) Pty Ltd
Sydney • Auckland • London • Cape Town
1/66 Gibbes Street Chatswood NSW 2067 Australia
218 Lake Road Northcote Auckland New Zealand
86 Edgware Road London W2 2EA United Kingdom
80 McKenzie Street Cape Town 8001 South Africa
Copyright © 2010 New Holland Publishers (Australia) Pty Ltd

National Library of Australia Cataloguing in Publication entry

Rogers, Sheridan.
Mini chef / Sheridan Rogers.
9781742570273 (hbk.)
Cookery--Juvenile literature.
641.5123

Publisher: Fiona Schultz
Publishing Manager: Lliane Clarke
Designer: Emma Gough
Project editor: Rochelle Fernandez
Proofreading: Kirstie D'Souza
Photographs: Graeme Gillies
Cover photograph: iStock
Food stylist: Amanda Biffin
Production Manager: Olga Dementiev
Printed by Toppan Leefung Printing Ltd (China)

10 9 8 7 6 5 4 3 2 1